Words of

# DR. FAD:

"Rid your mind of all the clichés about success. 'Build a better mousetrap, and the world will beat a path to your door.' Forget it! Make a better mousetrap and the world will YAWN! The really *big* money goes to the person who comes up with something completely different. Something entertaining ... and preferably useless."

———————

"The Wacky Wallwalkers have absolutely no social significance. That's why people buy them—*and* Mood Rings, *and* Pet Rocks. They're so dumb, people find them irresistible."

———————

"If there were more fads, there probably would be a lot fewer psychiatrists. Instead of paying for $100-an-hour therapy sessions, you could just lock yourself up in a room with a few Wallwalkers and a Slinky for a couple of hours. When you came out, you'd be fine!"

# How to Create Your Own Fad and Make a Million Dollars

**KEN HAKUTA a.k.a. DR. FAD**

with CATHERINE WILLIAMS and MARGARET B. CARLSON

AVON BOOKS  NEW YORK

AVON BOOKS
A division of
The Hearst Corporation
105 Madison Avenue
New York, New York 10016

Copyright © 1988 by Ken Hakuta
Cover photographs by Teresa Zabala
Published by arrangement with William Morrow and Company, Inc.
Library of Congress Catalog Card Number: 88-2732
ISBN: 0-380-70878-7

First Avon Books Printing: July 1990

AVON TRADEMARK REG. U.S. PAT. OFF. AND IN OTHER COUNTRIES, MARCA REGISTRADA, HECHO EN U.S.A.

Printed in the U.S.A.

RA    10   9   8   7   6   5   4   3   2   1

I dedicate this book to my father,
who taught me all
the things that matter.

# Contents

# Appendices

# One

# Dr. Fad's Wacky Walk to $20 Million

> *Making millions from a fad idea looks like fun and it is. But there's a method to the madness.*

Dr. Fad was born early in the evening of Sunday, October 10, 1982.

I didn't realize this until several months later, about halfway through making my first $10 million on the Wacky Wallwalker. But that evening marked the end of my life as the mild-mannered owner of an import-export business and heralded the beginning of my career as the leading marketer of fads in the country. Three years into my new life, I would have sold sixty million toys, one of the largest quantities of a toy ever sold in the United States.

It all began with a package from my parents in Tokyo for my sons, Justin and Kenzo, who were one and three years old at the time. Tucked in among the picture books and toy soldiers was a gummy piece of rubber with eight little sprouts sticking out. It was called "Taco," which means octopus in Japanese.

I asked my kids to let me look at the Taco. I threw it against the wall. It took to the wall and stuck there for a second. Then it came alive, shuddered, let go, flipped over, grabbed the wall again, wriggled, lurched downward, shimmied, and expired.

I was fascinated by this object that could amuse a three-year-old (Kenzo loved throwing it against the wall) and an adult—it went against expectations by coming alive and walking down the wall.

When the Taco arrived, I had no experience or interest in toys. I was exporting Teflon ironing board covers to Japan and importing karate uniforms from Korea, among other things. It was a respectable and lucrative business, although quite ordinary.

Before starting the export business, I had been a project evaluation officer at the World Bank. It was a serious job—suit, tie, wing-tip shoes, an office with a window. I went to India and Sudan to look at billion-dollar power projects and decide whether we should throw in another couple of million.

I didn't want to be stuck in a safe job at the World Bank for the rest of my life, so I went back to school to get my M.B.A. But a Harvard M.B.A. turns out to be a ticket to the kind of life I had left at the World Bank. It's perfect if you want to land a job in middle management at IBM, with a crack at a vice-presidency before you're forty.

The $75,000-a-year offer and a title were pretty tempting, but something told me that becoming part of a big corporation wasn't the way to spend my life. The World Bank had soured me on the desk-and-paper-clip mentality.

Instead of accepting an offer from Goldman, Sachs, I decided to go into business for myself. I rented desk space in a friend's office in Washington, D.C., for $100 a month and hung out a shingle saying import-export. I didn't know what I was going to import or export at the time, but I knew it was a safe alternative to Goldman, Sachs. I knew I would be able to find something people in Japan would want that Americans had and things Americans would want that the Japanese had. I would be in the middle.

So there I was, sending ironing board covers and cat food to Japan, karate uniforms to America, living the comfortable life. You go around saying you're in the import-export business and people are impressed. Maybe I wasn't going to make my mark in the world by introducing a country to the wonders of Teflon-coated ironing board covers, but I had some money in the bank and I was my own boss.

That was my state of mind before I laid eyes on the Wacky Wallwalker in 1982. It is the state of mind of most people in the world. The tendency in life is to do the prudent, sensible thing, be momentarily amused by something silly like this goofy rubber thing, toss it back to the kids, and get back to serious matters like that article in *The Wall Street Journal* on convertible debentures.

But I didn't go back to my *Wall Street Journal*. I was too intrigued. This rubber eight-legged creature that exists to be thrown against a wall or a window or a mirror, that has no other purpose in life but to climb slowly down a wall, captured my imagination.

The little critter kept nagging at me. I kept hearing a voice saying, "What if? What if?" I told myself surely someone else has snapped up the rights to this toy. I took comfort in that assumption, because it meant I wouldn't have to follow my instincts with all the risk that entailed. So I didn't drop everything right away and throw over ironing board covers and cat food for a wad of rubber.

But I did decide to make a few phone calls. What did I have to lose? Over the next three days

I called my parents to find out where they had bought the Taco. Then I called that store to get the name of the manufacturer. Then I called the manufacturer.

Three phone calls later, I had learned that the U.S. rights were up for grabs. Not that I had the money to buy them, but there they were. I had taken that first step. While part of me was happy to find rights available, another part was alarmed. If only I had the nerve, I could do something.

That the Wallwalker hadn't been snapped up also worried me, on the Groucho Marx theory of not wanting to be a member of any club that would have me. If the Wallwalker was as good as I thought it was, why was it still out there? What did it mean that the American toy companies in their infinite wisdom had seen fit to ignore it?

I wisely put the latter worry aside. Big corporations often make big blunders. They think big, so they miss the small things. Working nine to five, they miss the million-dollar idea that comes across the desk at five-thirty. Experts at playing it safe, they commission marketing studies and focus groups and demographic analyses to protect themselves.

I was convinced by this time that the Wallwalker was a great thing and I could make a go of it. I didn't have the handicap of corporate-think, but I had some other handicaps, like money. I didn't want to take on any partners, and I didn't want to buy the rights and import a few Wallwalkers, only to sell the rights to Mattel.

I called the Japanese manufacturing company again and offered them a deal I hoped they wouldn't refuse. I said I would order and pay for in sixty days' time three hundred thousand octopuses—a commitment of $120,000—in exchange for the worldwide rights to the toy. I was operating in fantasyland at this point because I had neither $120,000 nor any assurance that I would ever sell three hundred thousand of the things. I only had my belief that I could turn this toy into a fad.

The steps I took to keep from going $120,000 into debt and to end up $20 million to the good instead is the subject of this book. Contrary to what most people believe, fads are made, not born. It's true you have to have that captivating product, but what happens after that is cold, hard strategy.

It takes more belief than Hasbro has in G.I. Joe, more than Mattel has in Masters of the Universe, because you don't have their marketing muscle. But you have what they don't: a product you love and no bureaucracy holding you back. You are operating alone, like Willy Loman with his shoeshine and his smile, bucking the odds. I had the public on my side, the media rooting for me. I also had the sense to learn fast, to use some of the principles I picked up at business school, to discard others, and to make up new ones.

I'm going to tell you what I learned. Until I came along, no one had ever made a systematic study of how fads become fads, how some ideas go on to make a million dollars and others fade into oblivion. I get thousands of calls a month on my Fad Hotline from people who have experienced the moment I had when I asked my kids for a look at their new toy. It's not the same wad of rubber, but it's something equally captivating. There are a million stories out there about the great idea someone had. But only a few people go on to make the fortune I did. This book will tell you how to take that idea that keeps you awake at night and turn it into a million dollars.

I'm going to tell you how to distinguish between a genuine fad and just another product on the shelf, how to get started once you have the right idea, and how to run with it when it gets going. I'm going to show you how to get the right people on your team, how to work your way from the local newspaper to the *CBS Evening News*, how to get your product from prototype to the shelf at Bloomingdale's, and how to keep your fad alive when it begins to flag. I will guide you through the shark-infested waters of pushy distributors and hit-and-run knockoff artists. And I will teach you how to make your fad live forever.

Stay tuned.

# The Wacky Wallwalker Chronology

| | |
|---|---|
| *October 10, 1982* | Package for Kenzo and Justin from my parents in Japan arrived containing the octopus toy called Taco. Fell in love. |
| *October 20, 1982* | Called the manufacturer in Japan. Ordered three hundred thousand Wallwalkers, agreeing to pay within sixty days. |
| *October 30, 1982* | First shipment arrived. Xerox-copy directions and package toys in little plastic bags at home. |
| *November 5, 1982* | Started selling Wallwalker at gift shops and newsstands in Washington, D.C. |
| *Mid-November 1982* | Applied for trademark for Wacky Wallwalker name. |

| December 1, 1982 | Secured exclusive distribution rights to toy in North America. |
| December 24, 1982 | *Washington Post* Style Section article on toy. |
| December 27, 1982 | *CBS Evening News* segment on toy. |
| First week of January 1983 | First large air freight shipment of Wallwalker to United States arrived. |
| By January 15, 1983 | Orders obtained for seventeen million toys. |
| By end of January 1983 | Retailers guaranteed payment. |
| February 1983 | Obtained worldwide rights to Wallwalker toy. |
| Mid-February 1983 | Met NBC executives at Spago in Los Angeles. |
| April 1983 | *Time* magazine profile. |
| April 1983 | Began working on NBC cartoon special on Wallwalker. |
| May 1983 | MGM/United Artists called. Bought 50,000 Wallwalkers to use in promotion of James Bond movie *Octopussy*. |
| June 1983 | Wendy's called about offering Wallwalker as premium for 99 cents with the purchase of french fries. |
| July 1983 | Wendy's Wallwalker promotion began. |
| December 1983 | NBC Wacky Wallwalker TV special aired nationally. |
| December 1983 | *Life* magazine profile. |
| May 1984 | Toy factory set up in Korea to supply Kellogg. |
| June 1984 | Applied for patent on ingredient of toy. |
| June 1984 | Stopped selling Wallwalkers at retail. |

| | |
|---|---|
| *September to December 1984* | First Kellogg Wallwalker promotion. |
| *September 1985* | Started Fad Hotline. |
| *January to April 1986* | Kellogg's second Wallwalker promotion. |
| *January 1986* | First Fad Fair held in Detroit. |
| *January 1987* | Second Fad Fair held in Detroit. |
| *October to December 1987* | Kellogg's third Wallwalker promotion. |
| *November 1987* | Third Fad Fair held at Sheraton Centre in New York. |
| *January 1988* | *The Dr. Fad Show* premieres on CBS. |
| *December 1988* | Fad Fair held at Sheraton Centre, New York. |

# Two

# What IS a Fad? It's Not a Better Mousetrap

*A fad is something everyone wants yesterday and no one wants tomorrow.*

If you want to make it big in the fad game, you have to rid your mind of all the clichés about success. Take that old favorite: "Build a better mousetrap, and the world will beat a path to your door." Forget it. While making improvements on an existing product may earn you a little money from the few people who appreciate the innovation, the really big money goes to the person who comes up with something completely different.

I talk to people all the time who are spending all their creative energies trying to come up with things that are 10 percent better than what's already out there. I tell them, "Make a better mousetrap and the world will yawn."

If you look at the fads that have been runaway successes you'll see that a true fad has little utility beyond its entertainment value. Think of the Mood Ring, the Pet Rock, the Slinky, Silly Putty.

Don't get me wrong. Useful ideas have their place in the world. VCR's, transistor radios, and the Walkman are useful ideas that eventually became nationwide success stories. But these are more innovations than new products and in general have big companies and substantial advertising behind them. Also, while these products now have huge market penetration, the products built their markets systematically. The first VCR manufactured by Sony came out in the 1960s. It wasn't until the mid-1980s that it reached 50 percent penetration of households in the United States.

It's generally useless items that sweep the country all on their own: no advertising, no marketing plan, no big corporation, no technological innovation. It's an original product. Think of it this way. The VCR in your home today is a vast improvement over the one Sony put out twenty years ago, or you wouldn't have bought it. The VCR is not a fad. It's a technological advance that has won converts the more technologically advanced it becomes. And it is still being improved.

A fad isn't an innovation, and it doesn't change throughout its short life. The Pet Rock the first person purchased is the same as the one the last person to get in on the fad purchased. There is no improved version of the Pet Rock.

To sweep the country, forget being innovative about existing things and think original. I hear all sorts of ideas for better can openers, better corkscrews, and, for some mysterious reason in what amounts to a national obsession, better toilet seats. In the past year alone, I've probably heard of more than thirty ways to improve the toilet seat— better ways to open them, better ways to close them, better ways to shape them (from animals to lips); there are ones that are fur-covered, ones that light up.

That doesn't mean you can come up with a useless item, then sit back and wait for the world to beat the proverbial path to your door. What if the guy who thought up the Pet Rock idea did that? Do you think people would have called him up and said, "I hear you are selling rocks in boxes; I'll take ten gross"? This is where creative marketing comes in. If you come up with something that's useless and promote it the right way, everybody will have to have it yesterday, even though they get up the next morning and wonder why they bought it. When something is useless, you don't have to be bothered convincing your audience they need it. They don't. Get right up front with that.

The best fads are like jokes. You laugh when you find out about it. It can be a dumb joke like the Pet Rock, it can be a sight gag, or something that absorbs the attention span a little longer, such as Rubik's Cube. By the way, if Rubik had listened to the so-called experts, you'd never have heard of his cube. Robert L. Shook, author of *Why Didn't I Think of That!*, pronounced Rubik's Cube "just another puzzle that will never go."

Most fads that really fly, if not completely useless, have utility as a small part of their appeal. They are fun first, a statement of something second, and useful third.

Take an item that doesn't so much change a product as change the public's perception of it. An example of this is the Swatch, which made watches fun, cheap, and fashion-conscious. This went against the prevailing wind at the time, which was that watches were expensive, serious status symbols, as in Rolex; or were dull, inexpensive items, like Timex.

That Timex let Swatch snatch its market is an example of the mentality that dominates large corporations. Timex just didn't think up something that would make watches fun. They couldn't bring themselves to do it, even though their market share was slipping from those salad days when John Cameron Swayze captured the public's imagination with ads showing a watch being abused. Remember the frogman diving off the precipice, down into deep, deep ocean, and coming up twenty seconds later with the Timex still ticking? That was new and daring for its day, and Timex sold like crazy.

Swatch is the Timex of the 1980s. They only incidentally tell time. Swatches mostly make statements: I'm fashionable and I don't need to spend a lot of money to be that way. It says I'm secure enough not to have to lay out $6,000 to have a status symbol on my wrist. It says I'm not dull. Peripherally it says, "I don't have to know exactly what time it is. I have people for that sort of thing." Swatch says millions in the bank for the tiny Swiss company that thought up the idea.

Then another company came along and changed even further the way we think about watches. It's Le Clip, and rather than wear its inexpensive fashion timepiece on your wrist, you can clip it anywhere, from your lapel to the visor in your car.

What the *Fortune* 500 don't think up is to the fadster's advantage. They don't think new, they don't think daring, and they certainly don't think fun. They must chug stolidly forward while making even the tiniest change in direction.

Then there are food and toy fads, which are almost always more fun than they are useful. Nobody needed the Hula-Hoop. And no one needed another form of fast-food chicken until Chicken McNuggets came along. McDonald's wanted to get a piece of the chicken business but didn't want to compete with Colonel Sanders and his barrels of legs and thighs. So they came up with a completely new way of making chicken—in finger-size, boneless morsels—called them McNuggets, and clucked all the way to the bank.

Consider the chocolate chip cookie. At one time, cookies were either baked at home, involving time and effort, or bought in packages tasting like the bag they were sold in. Then suddenly cookie stores were popping up on every corner. No one had ever thought of selling cookies one at a time like ice cream cones in store front operations until Amos, who's now Famous, and all his imitators set up on the street and gave us what Mom doesn't have time to make anymore.

What Nabisco missed, and Mrs. Fields and the other cookie entrepreneurs took advantage of, was change, and the transient nature of people's tastes and buying habits these days. In fact, the *Fortune* 500 would do a lot better if they would realize that a lot of marketing these days is fad marketing. No one wants to be buying what the masses are buying. Everyone wants to be the first with a trendy item, and consumer loyalty to one brand is rare. Our parents found a product they liked and stuck with it for life. Everything from Chevrolets to Old Dutch Cleanser was bought and bought again, loyally, for decades.

Not so for this generation. We switch from Chevrolet to Ford and, to our parents' horror, Volkswagen and Honda. We are ready to try the new product on the block in a second. Look at ice cream, for example. About ten gourmet ice cream companies have started up in the past five years, but consumption has stayed about the same. These newcomers eat into the sales of the established companies, and the only way to recoup market share is to adopt the quick-hit techniques of the upstart competitors.

A couple of years ago the Dove Bar swept the country, really ripping into Breyer's sales. The Dove Bar is not something Breyer's couldn't have thought of if they were of the fad mentality. What's something new we can do with ice cream that doesn't come in a half-gallon package? They are playing catch-up now with Bon-Bons, a chocolate-covered vanilla ice cream, but they really gave away that premium ice cream bar market to Dove without even trying. And now Häagen-Dazs is coming up fast with their own supermarket bars.

Changing existing products that are mass-market items can have the same effect as a fad. Take something everyone uses, like toothpaste. Procter & Gamble, the largest personal-care products maker, really missed the boat on natural tooth-paste. Anyone who had lived through the environmental and fitness booms could have predicted that one. Instead, some guy in Maine beat them to the punch with "Tom of Maine's All Natural Toothpaste." It doesn't have any additives or sugar, just natural flavoring. Tom has now come out with a variety of flavors—cinnamon, clove, spearmint. No moss growing on his teeth. But Procter & Gamble could have been in there. With their marketing muscle, they would have had all the shelf space to themselves with a hot fad item.

The changes you make don't need to be useful. They only need to be fun. Take the toothpaste pump. This was a good attempt to make a sexy change in a standard product. Sales rose sharply for Colgate, which did it first. Who is to say that a toothpaste with a pump is any better than one without? The important thing is that it is different. If I were into toothpaste, I would have done the pump; a year later, an aerosol can. Then a year later, I would do bubble gum toothpaste that lets you brush your teeth and blow bubbles at the same time.

So far the big companies haven't absorbed the fad mentality. Otherwise Coca-Cola would have thought up designer water instead of fiddling with the flavor of Coke and leaving the huge bottled-water market to foreign companies such as Perrier.

When trying to launch something new you should do a little research to make sure your idea hasn't already been tried. You would be surprised at the number of calls I get from people on the Fad Hotline telling me what a great idea they have. These people tend to be on the intellectual side—a lot of fad inventors are—and they have been sitting in their easy chairs just thinking, sometimes for years. One guy called up to tell me about blinking lights you could attach to your car to indicate which way the car was about to turn. Another thought a machine to answer your phone when you aren't home would be a great innovation. These are great ideas to someone living in a convent.

Let me tell you something else that *definitely* is not a fad. Whatever you do, don't sink your life's savings into cliché items. I walk into souvenir and gift shops all the time and feel sorry for the guy who thought up the item that consists of a "stick in the mud." Or how about a bottle of "hot air" or a "losing your marbles" paperweight? These clichés have name recognition but are lifeless. If it was ever funny to see a skull full of marbles with a few dribbling out, it isn't anymore. Forget it.

The same goes for gadgets that surprise us because they go against our expectations. A piece of rubber that turns from blue to orange when you touch it is interesting, but interesting only once.

You will not care about it again. There is no ongoing charm and no fun to it.

The same goes for gadgets that do one thing exactly the same way all the time, such as a windup toy that does backflips. Watching a Wallwalker is like watching a cat, something alive, because it doesn't do the same thing over again. Unpredictability is its hallmark. You could say the same thing about Silly Putty. The face you lift off the comic strip page always stretches in a different way. Both the Wallwalker and Silly Putty have an element of human interaction. It matters what you do to them. They can capture the imagination because they take some imagination.

Natural phenomena are not fads, so pass on any schemes to capitalize on such events as Halley's Comet. Besides lack of shelf life (meaning total amount of time its interest is held), most of us have little enough control over things in our own backyard, much less what is going on in the fifth dimension. A lot of shirts have been lost on comets, eclipses, hurricanes, and similar developments.

Like natural phenomena, historic events are out. I know of only one that worked—the Miss Liberty Styrofoam crowns—and that only in midtown Manhattan. I get hundreds of calls from people who spend every waking minute trying to figure an angle on the five-hundredth birthday of the discovery of America in 1992. These people would do better to put their money in a passbook account.

I'm happy to say that the Wacky Wallwalker definitely fits into the useless category. It just crawls down the wall. And it does that fairly well. But there wasn't a crying need out there for something that crawls down the wall. Somebody asked me once, "Well, what is the social significance of the Wallwalker?" Now, I hear a lot of dumb questions, but that's about the dumbest. The answer is, of course, there is no social significance to Wallwalkers. It's just kind of fun to watch one for a couple of minutes. That's it. Nothing more serious than that. That's why people buy them, and Slinkies, and Mood Rings, and Pet Rocks, something that was so dumb a lot of people found it irresistible.

If there were more fads, there probably would be a lot fewer psychiatrists in the world. Instead of paying for $100-an-hour therapy sessions, you could just get yourself a couple of Wallwalkers and a Slinky and lock yourself up in a room for a couple of hours. When you came out, you'd be fine.

# Three

# Take the Money and Run: Unconventional Ways to Finance Your Fad

*If you're always ready to deal, you can turn anyone you meet into a banker.*

People come up to me all the time and say, "Gee, Ken, it must have cost you a lot of money to get the rights to the Wallwalkers for the United States." I say, "No, it hardly cost me anything."

And it didn't.

You might have to pay more for the rights to your fad than I did for the Wallwalker—zero—but it doesn't have to cost you much. And whatever it does cost, you can pay in a variety of nontraditional ways. Use your credit card creatively. Sometimes you can get money from the bank by using unconventional means. This doesn't mean armed robbery, but it also doesn't entail putting on a suit, going to the loan officer, and asking for a loan so you can go out and manufacture wads of rubber. He will laugh at you.

But I didn't know this when I first started out, so I went to my banker anyway the week after the Wallwalker made its appearance on my doorstep. I thought seeing him was a good idea because he had previously been willing to bankroll some ironing board covers and cat food.

We went to a restaurant and I said, "Tom, what do you think of this?" showing him the Wallwalker. Not much reaction. We weren't close enough to a

25

wall for me to throw the thing, so I put the beer bottle on the opposite side of the table and made a perfect pitch. The bottle wasn't the ideal surface, but the Wallwalker grabbed hold once, turned over, and grabbed again. I said, "I'm so excited about this little item that I am going to throw everything I have into it." He said, "You must be crazy." And he didn't lend me a cent.

Surprisingly, I still bank with Tom. That's fortunate for him, because now I'm a large account. I stuck with him because I didn't take it personally when he turned me down. He was just behaving conservatively, the way bankers do, and I was being an unrealistic fad entrepreneur. No banker in his right mind will ever finance a fad item. Don't even bother to fill out the forms. When you get to the line about what you need the money for, you will have to leave it blank. What would I have written, "To pay for a shipment of three hundred thousand rubber octopuses that walk on the wall"?

I wouldn't finance a fad if I were a banker, even if the loan request came from a regular customer. *Especially* if the request came from a regular customer. I would reconsider my entire association with him. "This guy is going funny on me. Maybe I should reduce his line of credit." So you end up worse off than you were before.

So what can you do? It's really all a matter of using what's available. You don't need me to tell you to lean on friends. You might be surprised how many want to get in on something different if it doesn't entail too much risk. Barry Gibson, who launched Celebrity Dirt, had no backing at all from his bank. He was a truck driver in Lansing, Michigan, living from paycheck to paycheck. He didn't ask me how to finance his project. He knew what to do. He called all his friends—he was lucky, he had quite a few. They all chipped in $100 or so each. This paid for the tolls and gas and motels to get him to Joan Collins' backyard in California. Fortunately, he already had the truck.

Another way to raise finances is to use as many credit cards as you can to stretch a line of credit. Go to ten different banks and apply for MasterCard and Visa. Then get $500 on each of your twenty credit cards. Everybody will give you that. You don't want to draw down on them one at a time because they will all find out. You draw down on all of them on the same day. Then you have $10,000, which is enough to finance a lot of your operation. If you have a hot fad, you worry about paying it back later. That's tomorrow's problem. You have today's problem to worry about. Remember, in a fad, timing is everything.

Similar to the credit card approach is getting a line of credit at ten banks for $2,000 or $3,000 each. You can get about $30,000 that way.

Keep in mind that a lack of money is no obstacle. A lack of an idea is an obstacle. Sometimes having money can work against you. It limits you. Better to have no money at all and have big ideas than to have $50,000 and be limited to $50,000 ideas.

I wasn't limited in that way. I had no money, so I could have the million-dollar idea instead of the $50,000 idea. When I persuaded the Japanese manufacturer to give me the Wallwalkers on credit for sixty days, I then had to convince the large chain stores in the United States to pay for the things on delivery—unheard-of in American retailing—to pay off the manufacturers before the sixty days ran out. This is when you have to love your fad, believe in it to the hilt, or you won't be able to pull it off. You are going out on a limb on both ends—with the people who are making the things and the people who are going to sell them for you.

My major form of financing, other than credit cards, was convincing the Japanese manufacturer to give me a $120,000 line of credit. In effect, he became my bank, my largest creditor. How did I get him to do this? I did all of it over the phone. I had some business references, which he checked. But largely I relied on his trust and his desire to sell more octopuses. He was willing to take some risk for the gain of selling three hundred thousand in one order. I convinced him that I would sell those three hundred thousand and more. That I would work that thing until it became the hottest-selling item in the United States. I helped convince him I was serious when I agreed to pay the cost of air freighting the Wallwalkers to America—about $20,000. Now, I didn't have to pay the air freight company immediately or all at once. The air freight company doesn't ask for money up front. Just tell them to ship collect and bill you, and they will.

It's quite surprising how many companies work on credit. Raw-materials suppliers and transportation companies are very slow in demanding payment. It is relatively easy to get credit with them, so that they turn into another bank for you. Very often you can start shipping on credit immediately. The worst-case scenario is that you do one piece of business with them, paying cash, and establish credit that way. Then they will bill you. These companies are also slow to bill, slow to collect, and don't cut off your account when you're late.

I used Flying Tiger Lines and Northwest Airlines to fly the Wallwalkers here. They gave me great credit. I was able to stretch them out as long as it was convenient to me. Best of all, I had this line of credit without finance charges. This gave me time to sell Wallwalkers and pay them with my earnings. It often takes them thirty to sixty days even to send a bill, and all this time you have an interest-free loan. Why do they do it? They want to get your business. And most businessmen are successful and pay their bills. I certainly did.

I also got K mart to agree to pay on delivery. Ordinarily, they pay sixty days after delivery or more. I was able to get this concession from K mart because the Wallwalker was already hot. This meant I was able to pay the manufacturer and the air freight—almost on time.

You are always negotiating terms. If it's your neighborhood boutique, tell them you will give them a 10 percent discount for payment on delivery. Usually they will accept. They don't have anything to lose. They don't have to take a second shipment if the first doesn't sell.

With distributors, you can also negotiate terms. I had a distributor who gave me a check for $50,000 because he wanted to get the Wallwalker before anybody else. He could sell high by being first. He wanted a guaranteed supply. If you're not that hot, you can still work out terms. Here, too, offer a small discount for getting paid upon delivery. You could offer a bonus: For every hundred dozen ordered, they would get ten dozen free. You have to be flexible here. The more successful you are in convincing all these links in the chain that you are going to be a very hot item, the better the terms you can negotiate.

I was working with smoke and mirrors at this point. Without an unshakable belief that what you are doing is going to fly, you can't get a department store to agree to buy something that doesn't exist and a manufacturer to make something for which there may be no buyers. I was so confident that this was the fad of the decade that I could say, "Here is my toy and here is what you are going to have to do to get it."

It's all negotiation. They don't really know you. How do you talk them into trusting you for $120,000 worth of merchandise? You have to make them beleve in you, and each person has his or her own style there. I was able to convince the Japanese manufacturer that I would pay him the entire amount due whether or not I sold a single toy. Because it was such a huge order, he was willing to take the risk and give me the exclusive distribution rights in return for my signing on the dotted line. He was no fool. He knew I was liable for the money whether or not I was putting up collateral. But in the end it was my belief in myself and my product that really convinced him.

By Thanksgiving 1982 I had borrowed the money I needed and established the necessary credit with my suppliers. Borrowing money takes courage and commitment. If I hadn't been totally committed to the Wallwalker, I never would have had the nerve to put myself on the line the way I did. It wasn't just my friends who pooh-poohed the idea, it was the best guys in the field as well. Even Richard Knerr, founder of Wham-O, the most successful fad merchandiser in history, told me he'd passed on a similar concept several years ago because he didn't see a market for it. If I'd listened to him, I might still be in the cat food business.

Four

# Name That Fad

> *Quickly, what is a Navistar? Bet you don't know and neither does anyone else. It doesn't matter if you're selling combines and threshing machines. But you have to be a lot better with names if you want to be the genius behind the next Hula-Hoop.*

Think if I had kept the name of the creature that arrived by mail that day: "Octopus." If you had the choice of marketing "Octopus" or "Wacky Wallwalker," which would you choose? More important, which would you buy?

It's all in a name. That's a great precept to go on when marketing a fad. Corporations can spend millions of dollars on naming or renaming themselves, yet they can afford to be dull; in fact, it's an advantage. Allegis (United Airlines) or Primerica (American Can) or Unisys (Burroughs and Sperry) prefer that their names not give away what exactly it is they do. Then they can do anything they want to.

But be vague with a fad and you're finished. Consider the "Photon" game. I asked at random among my friends to tell me what a Photon game was. Not one of them got it right. One guessed a camera, another a high-tech gizmo. No one guessed a game using lasers in which children strap sensors to their bodies and try to tag each other with beams of light, like bandits in the night. The Photon was a great game, but it never really caught fire.

Enter a smart marketing man who renamed the

product "Laser Tag," which, at once, explains what the toy actually is—an old-fashioned game of tag—and gives it a glitzy, high-tech image with the word "laser." It takes off like a rocket at the toy stores.

There is a very important lesson here. As a book is judged by its cover, so a fad is judged by its name. You can have quality—the laser tag game was always a quality item—but without the right name, it can fail miserably. If you slap an empty name like Photon on something—except a unit of intensity of light at the retina equal to the illumination per square millimeter of a pupillary area from a surface having a brightness of one candle per square meter, which is what it is—it will stay on the shelf, no matter how worthy a game it is.

A catchy name conveys information, amusement, and curiosity all at the same time. In this age of instant gratification and *USA Today* factoids, you have about twenty seconds to get your point across. A name that quickly and clearly sums up what a product is fits into the split-second attention span of the buying public. If you can make them smile, all the better.

You also have to shoot for high-name recognition. Something repetitive helps. Consider Coca-Cola. This soft drink was named back in those days when corporations didn't send out for experts to make up names like Exxon. The name described the product, and also had alliteration. Don't think this was lost on the Wham-O Corporation, the only company in America that specializes in fad toys, when it named the Hula-Hoop. And it's not accidental that Wacky Wallwalkers has three w's.

A name is particularly important for a product that isn't going to be advertised. The name on the package *is* your advertising. If the name doesn't convey the image of your product, what it is, and what it does, you're wasting the equivalent of a thirty-second spot on prime-time television.

Consider these great successes: the Hula-Hoop, Silly Putty, and Slinky. What they all have in common is that they say what they are, and they do it in an amusing way. People are hedonists at heart, and they are attracted to simple pleasures more than any other, from twirling a plastic, brightly colored hoop around their hips to slapping goo on a comic strip and twisting the picture out of shape.

Who would have thought that something as mundane as a Band-Aid could become a hot item? Not me, until I got a call on the Fad Hotline from a woman who had spent years looking for some everyday item that could be made more creatively. She decided on Band-Aids. She redesigned the old staple—made them into different shapes, some in the form of favorite storybook and cartoon characters. But the most important thing she did was to give these new-age Band-Aids a name that said what they did and could dry the tears of a child with a skinned knee at the same time. Owie Wowies struck just the right note, and now these funny Band-Aids are on their way to becoming a big marketing success.

Another item the world could have gotten along without went on to become a great success largely because of its clever name. A guy from Los Angeles called me with an idea for a new kind of can opener, but since it was an opener for flip-top cans, which don't require an opener, the guy had a problem.

The problem was solved with a clever name. He called his opener "Ladyfinger" and made it look like a woman's index finger, long nail and all. The message: No more broken nails if you use my product. The name established instant rapport with potential buyers—women who had broken fingernails opening the new flip-tops, or men who wanted to be sympathetic to their loss—and took note of a universal, annoying, albeit minor malady. A product that might have had no market went on to sell close to a million units in a few weeks. A buyer from K mart gave him an order for six hundred thousand within minutes of seeing it.

I knew I had to use the name of my toy to grab the public. When I received the first shipment of octopus creatures that slithered down the wall, I let my mind wander over the words that described its attributes: slimy, crawly, creepy, mushy. But none of these words captured the essence of this mass of rubber. The octopus was comical, and I wanted a word that captured that as well as what it was.

Throwing it up against the wall again and again, I realized what it did. It walked on the wall; it was a wallwalker. There is no such word as Wallwalker, and I am suspicious of made-up words—such as Primerica and its ilk above. But I decided to overlook that in this case because "wallwalker" was so descriptive. Although it wasn't a real word, it combined two real words. I then wanted a word that suggested how crazy it was and that also was alliterative. The Wacky Wallwalker was born.

There was a lot of criticism of my choice at first. Friends said Wacky Wallwalker was a tongue twister. That just confirmed my sense that it was the right name. A jumble of syllables helped describe the tumbling nature of the toy. Others felt it was too strange to get the necessary recognition. But being different is all right if it captures the feel of your product.

In naming your product, don't be afraid to be silly. Much better to be productively silly than soberly stupid, as the Photon people were. Those six letters are a waste of space on the package. Better to have left the package blank and arouse curiosity that way than to put on such a meaningless name.

# Five

# Getting Exclusive Rights

> You wouldn't share your first love with anyone else. Don't share your fad. Make it yours and yours alone.

Great fads can be started with products that already exist. I didn't have to invent the Wallwalker, I just had to invent a market strategy for it. But before I did anything, I had to get the exclusive rights to it. This is essential for any fadster because without these rights, you'll not only lose a lot of time and money, you'll also lose the whole thing. Competitors can easily come in and steal it. Without exclusive rights, you can do all the groundwork—setting up the business, transporting the goods, obtaining liability insurance, promotion, initial sales— for nothing.

There are different kinds of rights. From an inventor you can get an exclusive license to the product. Or you can buy the legal rights or patent that has already been secured. From a manufacturer you can get exclusive distribution rights to the whole country, to all of North America, to one region, or just to specific accounts, such as Woolworth, K mart, and Target stores, if that's all you want. But remember this: If the manufacturer is in another country—as was the case with the Wallwalker—then you want to become the exclusive importer. That's where the money is.

Securing rights can be easier than you think.

Take the case of the Frisbee. Richard Knerr and Arthur "Spud" Melin were two college friends with a small-time mail-order operation called Wham-O that sold mostly slingshots. One day at the beach in California they saw a disk fly through the air. It looked like fun, and these were two people who had dedicated their lives to having fun. They asked the guys playing where they got the disk and they said the Los Angeles County Fair.

Rich and Spud went to the fair and found the booth where the disks were being sold by a guy named Fred Morrison. He and his wife made a living going around to local fairs selling the thing. Spud and Rich negotiated exclusive rights to the disk right then and there and began manufacturing it. This was back in 1955. As a money-maker, it took a long time for the Frisbee to get off the ground, but after a couple of years it took flight. It soared in the sixties and has been flying ever since. This fad classic has made Rich and Spud very rich.

They weren't so lucky with their next discovery, the Hula-Hoop. It's hard to believe that the largest-selling toy ever—eighty million were sold in 1958 alone—wasn't a huge money-maker for Melin and Knerr. When a friend first brought them a bamboo exercise hoop from Australia, they knew instantly they had a winner. But after their experience with the slow-starting Frisbee they weren't prepared when the hoop took off almost overnight. Publicity turned the Hula-Hoop into a worldwide explosion before the rights to it had been secured. Demand for hoops soon outstripped production. Wham-O couldn't keep up. Sometimes this can be a good thing, creating the hard-to-get image that can further fuel a fad. But when you have no patent protection, it can be a disaster. More than forty competitors were able to flood the market and cash in on the fad they had created.

A similar experience happened to the creator and marketer of the Mood Ring, who also sought publicity before securing rights and was pushed out of the game by dozens of competing manufacturers. Timing is crucial: You can have a million-dollar idea, do everything right, but if you don't do it in the proper sequence, you could lose out.

A willingness to negotiate also is important. Unless you are buying someone's legal rights outright (assuming that the other party you are negotiating with is halfway intelligent), he is going to want something in return for the exclusive rights. If you are Sears, Roebuck, then you don't have a problem, but if you are just an individual or a very small company, you are going to have to prove to him that you are worthy of receiving the exclusive rights. This sounds intimidating, but it's not half as difficult as you may think.

For example, let's say there is a company in California that makes an electronic skateboard that is distributed in that state only. You see a market for it in New England and want to become the distributor there. So you contact the company. If the owner says, "I've never thought of selling in New England and nobody has ever asked me for those rights," he's a sitting duck. He has revealed himself. You have no competition. There is a chance he might just give you the rights for very little commitment. He might want you to give him a minimum order for, say, three thousand to thirty thousand, depending on the product. Or he might let you have exclusive rights on the condition that you sell thirty thousand skateboards a year, or lose the rights.

Most rights owners will want a minimum order and a sales commitment—in general, as high a minimum order and sales commitment as possible. You, of course, want the opposite. Once the company owner has stated what he wants, it's up to you to negotiate down. You want to have as small a commitment as you can get for the longest period of time. That way you have some room to build up a market. If you don't negotiate enough time for yourself, you will be fighting the clock. You don't want to be at the takeoff point—having developed demand for your product—just as your exclusive rights are ending. Then it turns out you have done all that work for some other guy.

# Six

# To Incorporate, or Not to Incorporate: That Is the Question

Any fool can incorporate but only a fadster can sweep the nation with his cockeyed idea. Incorporate if you must, but don't delude yourself into thinking that means you've launched your fad.

A question that always comes up—and not just with fads—is whether a budding business should be incorporated. People have heard about that wonderful notion "the corporate veil" and think it would be nifty to have one. Who wouldn't want a shroud to protect oneself and one's loved ones when the worst happens—personal-injury suits, bankruptcy, foreclosures?

What people who ask this question haven't heard as much about is that other notion, much beloved among lawyers, called "piercing the corporate veil." This is what happens when your car gets repossessed to settle the debts of the ABC Corporation. No one is so fooled by the "Inc." you have attached to your doings that your assets are forever immune from the debts you run up while pursuing the American dream.

My answer to whether to incorporate is to do what I did: Put it on the back burner. I didn't incorporate right away. In fact, my fad was a big success before I ever got around to it. My theory was that unless I knew the Wallwalker would be around for at least six months, it made no sense to go to all that trouble. Incorporating costs money. Even if you do it yourself, it will cost you money, and if you use a lawyer, it will cost you a lot of money.

One of the major reasons people give for incorporating is to save on taxes. You don't really save anything on taxes by incorporating. You can just as easily account for all your expenses on your own personal tax form as business expenses (on Schedule C). You avoid the possibility of double taxation (when the corporate profits are taxed when the corporation earns them, and again when they are distributed to you in salary or dividends). And you can deduct personal losses from other income. Corporate losses you just swallow.

Incorporation used to be a better deal before the Tax Reform Act of 1986, a decidedly corporate-hostile, human-friendly change to the tax code. There used to be a large difference in the tax rate on corporations and humans—humans paying about 24 percent more. The difference is negligible now. And if you factor in to your calculations the fact that you are more likely to sustain losses (at least on paper) than gain in your first year and that only humans, not corporations, can deduct them, it makes tax sense not to incorporate.

When you incorporate, you take on a number of obligations which can be very painful and time-consuming, particularly when you are trying to launch your fad. I just wouldn't have had time to file the quarterly statements required both at the state and federal levels, name a board of directors, call an annual meeting, issue stock, establish voting and nonvoting shares, draw up bylaws, and send out minutes of annual meetings that I also wouldn't have time to hold.

When I was young and foolish and still at university, I incorporated my tiny karate uniform business because I thought it would be fun to go around saying I owned a corporation. It was fun, in a subtle kind of way, until one day when I received a form from the state for my annual filing fee of $500. All the fun went out of the corporation at that moment.

If you don't do anything, the law will consider you a sole proprietorship. The only thing you have to do to operate your business that way is to load up on liability insurance (see Chapter 10: "Let's Get Legal") and pay your taxes.

Suppose you decide to incorporate. You are rich. We live in a litigious society where people who are not rich like to sue other people who are rich, whether they have done anything to warrant it or not. You don't mind if someone sues your company if he finds a fly in his soup at New Wave Foods, Inc., but you would like to keep the house, the stables, the pool, and the villa in the south of France safe from harm. Or perhaps you need to raise money through the issuance of stock. Or you don't want to be in this thing alone, but a partnership where every partner is liable for the acts and debts of every other partner scares the pants off you. Or fringe benefits applicable to corporations, like pensions, health insurance, company cars, and the like have appeal. As for double taxation, you decide to risk the suspicion of the IRS and pay everything the corporation earns (so that it has no taxable income) in salary and dividends to its president, you. Or perhaps you just like the trappings of office—corporate seals and running meetings according to *Robert's Rules of Order*.

Well then, incorporate, even though there are a heap of things you need to do.

- Decide which state to do it in. It doesn't have to be the one you live in. Delaware is a favorite because it has the simplest rules: It requires only one director (you) and doesn't insist on annual face-to-face meetings if there is more than one director. Writing back and forth or conference calls suffice. Also, it is harder to pierce a corporate veil woven in Delaware.

- When you decide where, I would then hotfoot it to the Yellow Pages and walk through the listings under "corporate services." There you will find companies organized to do nothing but file the papers that get you incorporated. Prentice-Hall, an imprint of Simon & Schuster, and the United States Corporation, both in New York, are two of the national companies. They say they do business with lawyers only, so that lawyers won't go after them for stealing their business. But you should be able to get the forms and information you want.

- These forms will tell you to file articles of incorporation with the secretary of state of the state in which you're incorporating. It's a boilerplate document and costs from about $50 to $350 to file, depending on how greedy your state treasury is. You need to state what the purpose of the corporation is ("to perform any act permitted under the laws of the state"), the name of a registered agent who can be served papers (this can be you), and the names and addresses of the incorporator (you). You then need to meet to elect directors and officers (in Delaware only one; three frequently in other states), decide what authority they have (not much), and adopt bylaws (keep them simple; you can get these from Prentice-Hall as well).

I consider all this a pain in the neck. But worse is complying with all the rules. If the major reason you have incorporated is to avoid personal liability and you get sued, the first thing the plaintiff's lawyer will do is pierce the corporate veil by showing that you didn't hold that quarterly meeting last year with a quorum of directors, or you didn't send out minutes or ever, ever affix that corporate seal to any document.

When it comes to one of the alternatives to incorporation—partnership—take a page from Nancy Reagan's book and "just say no" over and over again until the urge goes away.

As I said, I briefly flirted with incorporation in my zany, carefree youth, but I have never in my most madcap moments contemplated a partnership. Ask yourself if you really need your Uncle Arnold's money that badly. Is Rupert's way with a calculator that important that you are willing to go into business with him? In other words, do you really need a partner? When I was in business school, I was amazed at how people went into business in pairs, as if they were getting married. Maybe it was a substitute. There seemed to be no logical reason for doing it because very often two people with the same abilities and same lack of capital would go into business together, neither compensating for the other's weaknesses. You can go to dinner with your friends, show up at their kids' graduations, but you don't have to go into business with them. I'm not going to tell you how to form a partnership. It is so fraught with peril (if your Uncle Arnold gets drunk and runs over your Aunt Martha, you're liable) that you should run to a lawyer the second the idea crosses your mind and hope he talks you out of it.

Whether you incorporate or not, you need product liability insurance. No matter how unlikely your product is to cause injury, you must remember that there are always people out there ready to sue because Jupiter was misaligned with Mars the day he bought your product, which happens to be the same day he got a crick in his neck that just won't go away. The best approach to take is to plan on being sued and behave accordingly.

That means to get insurance. You can forget the lawyer, forget the public-relations expert, forget the receptionist, but you must buy the insurance. You will be sorely tempted not to buy product liability insurance when you find out how much it costs. Rates have hit the ceiling in the past few years as huge damages, particularly in medical malpractice suits, have prompted the insurance companies to raise their rates as much as ten times.

One thing I didn't skimp on was insurance. At first the coverage I needed cost $6,000 a year. That was in 1982. It now costs $80,000 a year, but I still opt to carry it.

There are ways to get around having insurance if you are dead set against it. There are otherwise intelligent individuals who "go bare"—have no insurance coverage. The $80,000 I am paying per year, they put into a self-insurance fund—and hope for the best. The advantage is that you can earn interest or invest the $80,000 if it remains under your control, which you can't do if you are paying it out in premiums. What I pay is gone forever. The disadvantage is that product liability suits can run into many millions of dollars. If you are just starting out—even if you conscientiously put the $80,000 aside—it will hardly be enough if disaster strikes. Without an insurance company to pay in the event damages are awarded, you will quickly go bankrupt.

There is one other way around the insurance conundrum. If you are doing business primarily with one manufacturer or distributor who already has product liability insurance, you may be able to arrange to be covered as well. For a much smaller sum than the $80,000 I am paying, you can arrange to get a rider that will cover you. Insurance companies are willing to do this because they already have a certain liability for the product as a consequence of insuring the manufacturer. They earn an additional premium without unduly increasing their exposure on the product.

One of the things you must do in connection with your own liability and because you want to be able to sleep at night is to have your product tested for safety. Many fad items fall under the regulation of the Consumer Product Safety Commission, which sets safety standards for all sorts of products, from toasters to trail bikes to childproof caps on medicines. The best way to find out if you are in compliance with the CPSC standards and to be prepared in the event you are ever sued for injuries your product allegedly causes is to submit your product to an independent testing laboratory for evaluation. That way, you have in writing that your product meets or exceeds safety requirements. Just as important, if your product fails the test, you have the opportunity to fix it. Part of the testing lab's service is to tell you how to bring your product into compliance. A list of independent testing labs and organizations is given in Appendix 1.

# Seven

# Getting Your Act Together

> *Forget the trappings of office. You're not running for anything or out to impress anyone. Get down to what's really important fast: selling the world on your idea.*

The most important advice I can give you once you have obtained exclusive rights to your fad is DON'T SWEAT THE DETAILS. One of the mistakes beginners make is to spend too much time on the nonessentials. As the maker of a fad, you don't have time for the nonessentials. Your fad could be over by the time you futz around with all the silly tasks waiting to eat up your time and energy if you let them.

I bring this up because fussing with details rather than thinking strategically is a trap many people fall into.

First of all, a fad doesn't require much in the way of a bureaucracy. Like artists and actors and other creative types, fad people can get away without a lot of structure. The trappings of the right business image—"a name on the door, a Bigelow on the floor," as Madison Avenue puts it—is something you can fortunately ignore. It's costly to run an office and peripheral to what your business is about. A receptionist, particularly one with a British accent, is a nice touch, one that impresses potential clients. But you don't have clients. You have customers who will be just as happy you aren't spending money on frills that will be passed along in higher prices. An answering machine will get the job done nicely.

Once you have an answering machine, you don't even need an office. To keep overhead down, the successful fad entrepreneur improvises in a way that turns his life into one big zoning violation. The family garage becomes a warehouse, the street in front of your house a loading zone, your kids an assembly line. The spare room turns into a storage and packing depot. My college roommate still complains about the stacks of karate uniforms that filled our room. Most of my staff for a million-dollar business consisted of me and my wife, and she was part-time. We worked out of our bedroom. At night we took crates of Wallwalkers into bed and watched TV as we cut up tiny slips of Xerox-copy instructions and stuffed them into small plastic goldfish bags from the pet store. Remember, the lower the overhead, the higher the profit ceiling.

There will be plenty of time to hire help when you know you have a fad. Many people ask me when that moment is. I had several false alarms, but now I know when the Wallwalker truly became a fad: It was New Year's 1983. The *Washington Post* piece had run and the *CBS Evening News* segment had run here and abroad. Suddenly I had several hundred thousand dollars' worth of solid orders. I had about a hundred phone calls backed up. I had limousines stacked up outside my house like 747s at Kennedy International Airport.

The plan I had for distribution became totally inoperative at this point. Stores that had Wallwalkers were deluged with buyers. They were sold out within hours. What was I going to do? I said to myself, "Well, maybe these are the fifteen minutes Andy Warhol said each of us gets. If that's the case, I better move fast."

That is when I took on a very small staff. Even so, I didn't get an office with a secretary. I hired some people to man the telephones (I had called the phone company and ordered two more lines). I hired a few people to take orders and be messengers. I paid these people on an hourly basis with no promises about how long the work would last. A fad can die anytime, and you don't want to be stuck. Remember, too, that if your fad takes off you have to be prepared to work harder yourself than you ever worked before. I had to make all the decisions, sift through the orders, talk to the factory, arrange delivery. I went to the airport personally to pick up my air freight shipments and make sure the order was complete and intact. That meant that for me (and my family) there was no Christmas, there was no New Year's. Everything had to wait. I knew that it wasn't a question of shifting from second to third gear but of changing my mode of transportation totally. I went into orbit.

Now for what you do need. Number one is an account with Federal Express (remember, every day of Fad Standard Time is a year) and a postage meter. It also helps to have a friendly neighborhood coffee shop (with a bottomless-cup policy) where you can conduct business meetings when you can't arrange to get together at the other guy's office.

By eliminating the office, you also eliminate all the other things that go with it: the power suit, the power coffee machine, the power ficus tree in the corner, and the power computer. The money you save goes straight into getting your message out there. Every cent that goes into a word processor to type the perfect correspondence is coming out of a trip to be on a talk show in Philadelphia.

When I first started, I figured that a typewriter was a basic requirement. I bought one, but after a few months it broke. Because I was so busy at the time, I never bothered to get the thing fixed and soon discovered that it was more efficient to write my letters by hand whenever I had five or ten minutes to spare and wherever I happened to be—waiting to see a buyer, stranded in an airline terminal, listening to Muzak while on hold.

At first I was concerned about what my correspondents might think. To my relief, I learned that goal-oriented businesspeople aren't judging you by appearances. Big companies are not looking for letters suitable for framing but for messages telling them that five hundred thousand red and white widgets will be delivered on time.

One day I was having lunch in Battle Creek, Michigan, with some Kellogg executives with whom I had done over $10 million worth of business. One of them told me about meeting with a competitor of mine at a business conference the week before. They were talking during a coffee break and this guy was going on about this Ken Hakuta guy whose Mickey Mouse operation doesn't even have an office or a secretary. "Would you believe it? I got a handwritten letter from Ken." The marketing executive of Kellogg who had agreed that day to buy several million Wallwalkers said, "Oh, yeah. Ken writes all his letters that way. Wish we could do that."

Not having the pressure of meeting a payroll and rent every month frees your mind to be creative. A fad will always be 90 percent creativity and 10 percent work. Once you have turned your inspiration into a product, you have to continue to dream up ways to place it before an admiring and free-spending public, not ways to do more elaborate cash-flow statements and spread sheets.

After an office and all its trappings, the next thing many people feel the need to waste money on is advice. The woods are full of con artists ready to take you for a ride. Look in the back of any business magazine and you will see what I mean. The pages are clogged with enticing ads offering to get your business idea off the ground for a small fee—anywhere from $500 to several thousand dollars. These people either do absolutely nothing—send you a sheaf of Xerox-copy notes—or get you into trouble with hackneyed advice that has nothing to do with your operation. It always involves ever-increasing fees.

One of these firms I checked up on begins by telling people to send their invention idea to them along with an evaluation fee. Then after they get your idea and have cashed your check, they send you a letter back saying how impressed they are with your idea and how marketable it is. For another $5,000 they will conduct a marketing survey. Fall for that one and you will get a Department of Commerce set of statistics on how many whatevers there are in the world and a letter offering to do another survey—say, of venture capital firms interested in backing ideas like yours—for another $5,000. This can go on until they run out of canned reports to send you or until you run out of money.

You might as well buy swampland in Florida. I have never heard of anyone being helped by one of these outfits. And I've talked to at least a dozen people who have thrown away more than $80,000 on this scam. Yet these ads appear in all the national business magazines.

Don't get suckered by these people. Check out information in your local library. Talk to local businessmen. Believe in your product. Work hard. Read this book. That's all the advice you'll ever need.

# Eight

# Taking It on the Road

> You've got nothing to lose but your dignity. If your attention-getting stunt would make P. T. Barnum blush, you're on the right track.

Now that you have your nonoffice equipped and have dispensed with the other nonessentials, you can get down to the real work: telling the world it can't live without something it still hasn't heard of. The very thought of a job this enormous is enough to send the most enthusiastic fadster back to bed for a week. So don't think about it, just do it. Start small. Break it down to manageable size, and do something every day.

Fads are like love at first sight—just one look and you're hooked. That's why your product has to be simple enough that you can show or explain what it does in fifteen seconds. Say, "It bounces." Not, "It bounces, then you can mold it into shapes, then if you leave it for three hours, you can paint it." The public response to that will be, "Wake me when it's over."

Once you have your fad distilled to a one-liner, you have to get out and around with it. You have to substitute shoe leather for a national ad campaign. You have to get your fad showcased in stores that establish trends and get the media to notice.

You also have to make sure people know what to do with your product. Who would have bought the Slinky if they just saw it sitting in its box on a shelf? If its creators, Betty James and her husband, hadn't hit the stores to show just what their Slinky could do, it never would have taken off.

No one would have wanted a Hula-Hoop unless they had seen for themselves how much fun it was. That's why Spud Melin taught his wife and kids how to use it. They all went off to the neighborhood park with their new toy, causing an instant sensation—local stores were deluged by buyers. After that Melin couldn't give the hoops away fast enough to the hundreds of kids willing to become walking advertisements. The same tactic worked on college campuses when Knerr and Melin made the rounds to show students what to do with their Frisbees.

Demonstrations at stores work just as well, and with a little effort you can get clerks to do the demonstrating for you. The best store for this is Bloomingdale's, which sets the pace for the rest of the retail industry. Treating retailing as entertainment, Bloomingdale's has become one of the highest-grossing department stores in the country. The rest of the industry takes its cues from Bloomie's.

You can't be everywhere showing people how much fun your fad is, so you need to get stores of this type in your corner. Clerks are part emcee. Give them a demonstration, make sure they are as good at using your product as you are, and leave the rest to them. Earn more goodwill by giving the clerks some items to keep for themselves. Remember, your product itself is the best promotional tool you have going for you.

This principle works in your own neighborhood, a more practical place to begin. That's how I got started. Your local K mart or Woolworth's isn't going to be interested at this point, but the small gift boutique is hungry for lively new items. Gift stores, smoke shops, and the cash register display at your local bookstore are all fertile ground. A lot of the trend stores, particularly gift stores, were willing to set aside space for customers to throw the Wallwalker.

Another advantage of going around to small stores is you can deal directly with the storeowners, who usually are on the premises. It's important to win them over as well as the sales clerks. As at Bloomingdale's, they become your biggest promoters. Keep in mind that they are captives of the store all day. They will appreciate you for livening things up and will be happy to have something to do besides dusting the shelves when business is slow.

You want the chains to be calling you. To attract their attention, aim for some specific targets— in addition to stores and events—that will have a ripple effect in the media (see Chapter 13 for a full discussion). You want the right people to be buying and talking about your fad. That's why I blitzed the newsstands and sandwich shops in the area around the office of the *Washington Post* where the journalists are likely to stop in for a pack of cigarettes (see Chapter 13). Also get the bartender at the corner pub to show off your fad.

I never needed to sell in Bloomingdale's. I got too hot too fast. You want Bloomingdale's for the display and demonstrations and the publicity that may follow. I got that from the boutiques and from the local equivalent of Bloomingdale's, Woodward & Lothrop. Woodie's, as it is called, is a high-end Washington, D.C., department store with a good sales force that can show off your product. Most cities have a store like Woodie's.

By the time Bloomingdale's wanted the Wall-walkers, I couldn't supply them. I had to make a choice between delivering 2 million to K mart or ten thousand to Bloomingdale's (that's about the ratio of department store orders to those of the big chains). Anyway, the best use of Bloomingdale's is to get a mass market. I was very fortunate to get a mass-market audience and a nationwide chain by other means. But if I hadn't been carried away by events and a very quick success, I would have gone there happily.

Another way of getting attention and initial orders for your product is through catalogs. If you can get into a really trendy one, such as the Sharper Image catalog, you are getting advertising you could never pay for. That's because the mailing list of the Sharper Image and catalogs like it—say, Neiman-Marcus—have the demographics: the urban professional thirty to forty-nine, with the considerable disposable income that all the companies are drooling over these days. One picture in there is worth several hundred thousand dollars' worth of advertising words.

If you're strapped for money and time and want to see if there is any interest before you sink any of either into a particular company, try calling first and talk to the person in charge of new products. But I don't think a voice over the phone is going to accomplish very much, even if you can get through. Fads speak for themselves, which is why I say just send it. At the very least, send a photo and a letter if you don't want to send the whole shebang. (I've included a list of addresses and phone numbers of these companies in Appendix 3.)

Direct mail can also be very effective. Getting into one of the brochures American Express sends out with its bills, for instance, gives you excellent exposure. If one tenth of 1 percent of the credit card customers order your product, your volume will be good. Even if they don't order, you will have put the idea of your product in their minds and they will be more likely to buy it when they see it in a shop. A company like American Express lends your product invaluable prestige.

If you go the catalog or direct-mail route, you have the additional bonus of having your customers finance your business. Rich Knerr and Spud Melin funded their slingshot fad (the one before they hit it big with the Frisbee) by not making anything until they had a prepaid order. Then they went down to the garage, where their girl friends and college dropout pals would make slingshots for a salary of one quart of beer an hour.

Like catalogs and direct mail, offering your product as a premium is a good way to expose it to the buying public without much risk on your part. At first glance it looks as if premiums aren't such a good deal, especially if you do it at the beginning. A company like Kellogg will offer you little more than cost. But they will more than make up for it in advertising. When Wendy's offered the Wallwalker for 99 cents with a purchase of french fries, I got $5 million worth of prime-time advertising. I chose to go the premium route at the end of the Wallwalkers' popularity to give them a new lease on life, but it may make more sense, advertisingwise, to do it at the outset if you have the choice.

Back in your own town, pick out events you know will be covered by the local media as I did—the Fourth of July Chamber of Commerce picnic, the Boy Scout jamboree, the opening of a new community center or shopping mall—and give away your product. Don't forget about donating your product as an auction item at school fundraisers. The auction catalogs are excellent free advertising. If you can, sponsor a contest. Frisbee tournaments were organized state by state as a way of starting and keeping alive that fad. A story in your hometown newspaper carries more clout than you might think. You would be surprised how many editors of big papers look at smaller newspapers for human-interest stories.

Your goal in all this is to get your product worn, drunk, eaten, driven, thrown, carried, and talked about by fashionable, trendy people, even if you have to give it away.

You should also consider traveling to Fad Fair, your best shot at national publicity. Even if you are just starting out and can't give your product away, a bit of ingenuity can get you media attention. They are there waiting for you. The stage is set. You just need to step into the footlights. See Chapter 18 for how to get on board.

# Nine

# Going It Alone or Going with the Big Guys

Which would you rather be: Colonel Sanders, who sold out his chicken empire and ended up slicing his profits to the bone; or John Y. Brown, who kept Kentucky Fried Chicken all to himself, became one of the wealthiest men in the country, was elected governor of the state, and married former Miss America Phyllis George?

One of the questions people ask me is "Should I sell my idea to a big company or run with it myself?"

When I found out that the rights to the Wallwalker were available, I had to make a decision fast. Should I buy the rights and manufacture or import the Wallwalkers myself? Or should I buy the rights and then sell them to a big company and have them market it? If I took the latter course, I would cut my risk and need for capital, but I would also make only a fraction of the potential profit from the toy. If I decided to try to keep the rights, should I form a partnership to buy them, spreading the risk over several people and raising capital at the same time? I would cut my risk but also my percentage. What should I do?

The answer for me was simple. I wanted it all. If I had sold the Wallwalker to a large company, I would have made about one thirtieth of what I eventually made. And when you're talking about one thirtieth of $20 million, you're talking about a pretty wide margin. Taking the licensing route would have been very tempting to most people, especially when a major toy company made a big offer, but the decision to take all the risk and see the thing through from beginning to end was the best one I've made in my life.

A lot of people point to the success story of Xavier Robert's Cabbage Patch dolls and Coleco as a good reason to license. But that fad was an anomaly. Not only was the doll priced higher than most fads, it's also rare that a large company has a fad success. At the height of the Cabbage Patch phenomenon, parents were lined up around the block to buy the dolls. This generated publicity, which was great. It also created the hard-to-get aura, which can make a fad even hotter. Coleco was brilliant at running the fad, but when it came to keeping it going, they weren't so smart. Instead of becoming an endangered species, Cabbage Patch dolls might have become American classics with the longevity of Barbie if Coleco hadn't milked them to death.

Then there's the example of Leonard Fish, the inventor of "Silly String," who licensed it to Wham-O about twenty years ago and got a royalty of 3 percent. Wham-O sold $20 million worth of Silly String. So Fish made $600,000. Big deal. He would have been better off if he had never walked into Knerr's office. Or if on the day he walked in Knerr had gotten up on the wrong side of the bed or just didn't get it, or had already licensed his quota of fad ideas that year, Fish would have been out on his ear but eventually up to his gills in money. Having no choice but to market Silly String himself, he would have made a lot more than he did.

Consider the guy out in Minnesota who invented Postit, those now ubiquitous pieces of note paper that have glue on one end. The inventor of Post-it got his idea when he was at choir practice and saw the choirmaster putting little pieces of paper containing conducting direction onto the sheets of music with tiny pieces of Scotch tape. He thought, Why not little pieces of paper with the Scotch tape already attached on one end? He went home and saw that it could easily be done—this is not what you call serious innovation. At this point he had the choice of starting his own company and marketing this item or turning it over to the company he happened to work for: 3M. He didn't want to take the risk, so he sold the concept to his employer. Instead of many, many millions of dollars, he got a bonus, a promotion, and a raise. That guy must be kicking himself now.

The reverse of this is Debbie Fields, the phenomenally successful owner of Mrs. Fields' Cookies. She started small—one store at a time—with a great recipe and a good line of credit. After a few stores it was clear she had a phenomenon on her hands. She could have sold out for millions of dollars, keeping a percentage. But she didn't. She risked everything, keeping total ownership. Not only did she not sell out, she didn't even franchise—sell her name and know-how to budding entrepreneurs, splitting the risks and the profits. She is now a multimillionaire with five hundred stores. She wouldn't be if she had sold out.

If you look at the short history of fads you'll see that I'm not the only one who figured this out. Nearly all fads have been created by individuals or very small companies that don't sell to large companies until the fad is over.

Consider the Slinky, something that's been around for over forty years and was started by a couple from Pennsylvania, Richard and Betty James. Richard discovered the marvelous properties of the Slinky when a large torsion coil fell from a shelf and began to move in a lifelike way. He knew immediately he had something very big. He quit his job, and the Jameses devoted all their time and energy to manufacturing, promoting, and selling the toy. Although they were inundated by offers from big companies to sell or license, they refused them all in favor of keeping complete control. As a result, in its long lifetime, the public has never been overexposed to the toy. Betty James, now a widow, runs the company and continues to reap the benefit of sole ownership—a benefit worth many hundreds of thousands a year. In a world of short attention spans, Slinky's staying power is legendary.

Lots of times, of course, it isn't a matter of making a smart decision on whether to license. Many times you aren't going to have the luxury of choosing between licensing with a big company or going it alone. You will be going it alone because no big company is willing to jump on board. Think: How many products does Mattel license every year? Hasbro? All the companies together do maybe five products a year. The chances are pretty slim for any one person; most times the fadster is on his own. But remember the positive side of this fact of life: You get to keep the bulk of the profits.

When you do embark on your fad alone, to the extent you keep the rights, you may still not be alone. You may need help. It's rare that any one person has the multitude of skills necessary to run a fad completely on his or her own. Indeed, no one at Mattel could do that. No one at IBM could do that. These people are taught marketing or product development, or finance, or distribution, and stick to that specialty. But a fad is one person. The guy in the garage doesn't have someone on the tenth floor to have a meeting with and decide what to do about promotion.

That being said, I still decided to do it all on my own. That's because I am moderately good at a lot of things, although not an A-plus in any one thing. Usually, one person is a D in financing, an F in distributing, and an A-plus in media. I'm a straight B in everything, which turns out to be enough to get the job done.

Ask yourself whether you are a specialist or generalist, good enough to cover a wide range of activities you need to pull off. Just as important, also ask yourself how important control is to you. It was very important to me that throughout the entire process I maintained 100 percent control, not just because I kept all the profits (although that was very important as well) but also because I remained the crusader, the Moses, of the product. I didn't have to sell any partners, or board members, on my fad. *I* was the fad. I didn't have to worry whether someone was as committed as I was. I didn't have to worry about whether I could talk anyone else into adopting my marketing strategy. I didn't have to worry about getting approval to build a factory or spending a couple of hundred thousand dollars on a lawyer to keep out the knockoffs. No board could tell me to price the Wacky at 99 cents when I wanted to price it at $1.29. Best of all, in my situation, as it turns out, no one could force me to milk the product to death.

The other great trap I avoided by keeping control was the specialist mentality. The sales rep, the public-relations man, the distributor, the lawyer are all going to look at the fad from their point of view. Imagine if the distribution people were in on the decisions. The minute Wallwalker sales dropped off at K mart, it would be finished from their perspective. I would have been hearing, "Ken, get out." They would be pushing to sell the next two million by dumping them on the market at any price. "Let's 'drop our pants,' Ken, and go to three for a dollar."

If the distributor has a 30 percent voting bloc, in the situation described above you drop your pants. Maybe you could get the marketing guy and the general counsel to vote with you and beat him, but that's unlikely. And once your product is on the "Three for $1.00 table" at K mart, it's over. Finished. Why would Kellogg use it as a premium in Rice Krispies, spending millions on advertising, if it's been keeping bad company in the bargain bin?

Even if you conclude you are like me—a control freak—you can still get help in some of these areas, short of licensing or taking on partners (remember hints on partnerships in Chapter 6). Licensing isn't an all-or-nothing proposition. Of course, you can sign one piece of paper and have a company like Wham-O do everything for you, like Silly String, or you can give up bits and pieces. In exchange for a percentage of the profits, you could, for example, get several distribution companies to handle marketing for you or hire a sales company, or join forces with a manufacturing company, instead of building your own plant. Then you are neither giving away voting shares nor giving away the whole ball of wax to a licensing company. You are just giving up some of your profit. You are buying expertise when you need it.

How you slice the pie if you decide to go this route is important. Think negotiable. Everything is negotiable at this stage. Start low, but realize that for the best people you are going to have to pay through the nose. Sometimes people are aghast when I tell them what I pay for some things, but the job gets done well and promptly. Next Tuesday in fads isn't good enough. You have got to get the person who can get results, who knows the ropes. You can't have someone learning on the job. No novices need apply.

Some people you just can't pay. This is a shame in some ways. Better to pay than to give up a percentage but, for instance, distributors don't work that way. Many want a percentage, and all you can do is negotiate. A big-time distributor is going to want a percentage *and* some exclusive rights. Don't do it. If you absolutely have to give away national distribution rights to get the best person, make it contingent on their producing and producing big. Get a guarantee. "You want the whole country," I say. "Deliver 10 million in sales in three months. In three months, if you do 9.9 million, it's bye-bye."

If the guy comes back and has 9.9 million, I say, "Close, but no cigar." You have to be tough because the distribution game is a jungle. Believe me, they'll stab you in the back if they can, and in this business it's considered legitimate, even admired. So you can't be a nice guy and hand over the money and say, "Well, 9.9 million. That's close enough." I don't like to play by these rules, but I've been in the business long enough to know that the only way to win is to be tougher than they are. I've shocked a lot of people because I don't seem like the ruthless type, but I only did what they do all the time, only I did it first.

So at this point, you have to say, "9.9 million. Well, that's not so close. You want an extension of a week to make it. Okay. But we jack it up to twelve million." They have no choice but to go along with you at this point.

This is why keeping control is so important. I had one distributor, one of the best in the business, and I really needed him. Behind my back he was trying to get a piece of my rights in exchange for distributing a huge shipment of Wallwalkers. His lawyer tried to slip a clause in our agreement that stated he would approve imports. This meant he could stop my imports from coming in the country at the port of entry. If I had been unhappy with his performance or for any reason wanted to replace him, I would have been stuck because he could stop my imports at the dock in San Francisco. Then where would I have been?

In another instance, I was shipping millions of Wallwalkers to an account. Logistically it was a huge operation. One of my distributors sent me his shipping clerk to help with the paperwork. But he double-crossed me and told the shipping clerk to make all the money payable to him, the distributor, instead of to me. I discovered this after the shipments had gone out and it was too late to do anything about it. So I was in the position of having him pay me instead of the other way around. He finally did after a lot of threats and long-distance yelling matches, but I still ended up losing $50,000 on the deal.

All types of people will try to pull stuff like that all the time, and you have to just keep saying to yourself, "I have got to keep control here." Again and again.

# Ten

# Let's Get Legal: Trademark, Copyright, Patent, and Other Formalities

> With all due respect, there is hardly anyone out there crazy enough to steal your idea.

Knowing when to hire a lawyer is a subspecialty in itself. Do it too soon and you are throwing money down a sinkhole. Wait too long and your fad may go up in smoke. Try to save a few bucks by retaining the rookie who handled the closing on your brother-in-law's condo and cry all the way to bankruptcy court.

The first thing to remember about lawyers is that a lawyer is not the first thing you need. Before you need a lawyer, you need an idea, a plan for executing it, the time and money to carry it out, and a commitment to see the whole thing through. Don't fall into the trap of getting a lawyer to make the project seem real. It won't ever be real if money you should be using to get started ends up in some attorney's wallet.

When people ask me when to hire a lawyer, I say if you have unlimited funds, get one and use him as an adviser. It's fun to go around saying, "I'll ask my lawyer about that." But if you don't have money to spare, you have to do a balancing act. You don't want to take money away from getting your fad launched to pay a lawyer's fee. And you don't want to get a lawyer before your fad is hot. If you get one and you never get hot, you have legal protection for something that died at birth.

Ask a lawyer when you should get a lawyer and he will say last week. They like to get in on things at the beginning. They get to make sure you do everything to the letter of the law and, not incidentally, to the advantage of their billable hours. Don't believe it. Lawyers want airtight contracts with every contingency covered, but only General Motors can afford that.

I didn't get a lawyer at the outset. I couldn't afford one, and the fact is I didn't need one. The legal protection I needed at the outset I got myself and so can you. You need a trademark, very easy to get. A trademark identifies or distinguishes your product from all the other products out there. For instance, Formica, Xerox, and Kleenex are three of the most successful trademarks, so successful that they have entered the common argot and are synonymous with the product.

By trademarking a name, you can be sure that no one else will be able to use it no matter how successful it becomes. Imagine how valuable the name Coca-Cola, and its shortened version Coke, is to that Atlanta company. In general, soft-drink lovers don't ask for a Pepsi when ordering a carbonated beverage containing caramel, caffeine, and bubbles. They ask for Coke, and therein lies a multibillion-dollar success story.

It's true that you don't actually have to get a trademark. I could have used the name Wallwalker without registering it. If someone else started using it, I could sue them for unfair competition and likely win if I could show that I had used it first. But why ask for trouble? For $160 you can register your trademark and give notice to the world that this mark is yours. That makes it impossible for anyone later to claim ignorance about it.

To register a trademark, go to the Office of Patents and Trademarks. The main office, in a suburb of Washington, D.C., is at 2021 Jefferson Davis Highway, Arlington, VA; tel. 703-557-3158. If you want to write, address your letter to Commissioner of Patents and Trademarks, Washington, D.C. 20231. They will send you an application and a booklet telling you exactly what to do. If you call the main number from a Touch-tone phone, you can listen to a variety of recorded messages that will tell you everything you need to know about registering your trademark.

I took the subway to Crystal City from my house in Washington and quickly found the Office of Patents and Trademarks. Two and a half hours later, I walked out with a trademark on the name Wallwalker. It was mine for all time.

Forget what you have heard about the bureaucratic indifference of government employees. The Office of Patents and Trademarks is a model of efficiency. It is organized around the principle that it is there to help businesspeople get the protections they need. The staff walked me through the process. The first clerk directed me to the files I would have to search to find out if anyone else had a trademark on the name Wallwalker. You don't want to use someone else's name because then it wouldn't be original, and originality is important in a fad. But more importantly, you *can't* use someone else's name. It's illegal. Fortunately, the Office of Patents and Trademarks has all the information on file that you need to find out if the name you want to use is available.

In doing the research on Wallwalker, I was crushed to find that General Mills had registered the name years before—not Wacky Wallwalker but Wallwalker, and that was close enough to raise problems. I went back to the clerk and told her what I had found. She led me to another book—a very important book, it turns out—that lists abandoned trademarks. Wallwalker was on the list. General Mills hadn't used the name for seventeen years and hadn't reregistered the trademark. I was lucky. So for $160 and a morning of research and filling out forms, I had gone from the owner of a Taco to the owner of the Wacky Wallwalker.

The other protection you need to get is a copyright. You can copyright just about anything—a book, a song, a dance, a blueprint, a design, any tangible object. What you can't copyright is just an idea. The federal copyright statute places discoveries, principles, systems, processes, and ideas outside the law. Once you've decided to copyright, you can do this with or without a lawyer.

Like a trademark, a copyright can be had without registering. Once I reduce my idea to a tangible form and affix "Copyright Ken Hakuta 1987" on the material, I have a copyright. That's all well and good until it comes time to enforce it. By registering, you let the world know when you came up with your design or whatever and exactly what it is. The document at the Copyright Office is absolute proof.

Registering a copyright couldn't be simpler. Call the Library of Congress in Washington, D.C., at (202) 287-9100 and ask for an application. Fill it out, and send two copies of what you want to have copyrighted (two models if it is a design) along with $10 to the Register of Copyrights, the

Library of Congress, James Madison Building, Washington, D.C. 20559. That's it. For $10 you have a copyright for life plus fifty years (your heirs get the benefit beyond the grave for the half century).

On the Wallwalker I have a copyright on the design of the toy. I didn't get that until January 1983, by which time it was definitely a fad. What registering does beside helping you sleep better at night is to give you the key to the courthouse—the right to sue, to get statutory damages (as opposed to having to prove actual damages), and to offer your registration as evidence of all the particulars surrounding your design. This eliminates your having to offer any other proof, such as when you actually went into business or began manufacturing. If you don't want to register with the Copyright Office because you are afraid some-one will look through the files and steal your idea, rest assured this won't happen. The Copyright Office won't let anyone but you or your lawyer ever see your "deposit" copy.

A patent is another matter, a much harder one. Don't run out and get one without thinking about whether you really need one or not. I get calls all the time from people who hardly mention their product. They just go on and on about the patents they have. So what? My nine-year-old son Kenzo could get a patent if he wanted. A patent itself has no value. It has value only when it is protect-ing the next Hula-Hoop.

Not to belittle your idea, but what I am about to tell you can save a lot of time, aggravation, and money: Most fads are too simple to need a patent. Patents are useful for protecting new inventions, better ideas, like a better mousetrap, or a stroller that folds. You don't need a patent for a product like a Swatch, for example. The watch mechanism has long been part of the public domain. The Swatch isn't original in that it doesn't use a new manufacturing prccess or any of the other things patents protect. Swatch only needed a trademark and copyright to protect its distinctive name and style.

Sometimes the material of a product, such as the material for Silly Putty or the sticky rubber material used in the Wallwalker, is patentable. The process used to make the raw material of the Wallwalker was new and needed protection. The reason the knockoffs didn't work as well is that although the toy itself could be copied—it wasn't a new invention—the material that gave the toy its unique property could not be copied.

If you decide to patent your fad, start by getting as much *free* information as you can by calling the Office of Patents and Trademarks at (703) 557-3158. A recorded announcement will give you the basic definitions—what a patent is, who needs to get one, and how to do it. You can get a book from the government on the subject; the book is an excellent primer. To obtain a copy, send $2 by check, money order, or by enclosing your credit card number (with its expiration date) to Superintendent of Documents, U.S. Government Printing Office, Washington, D.C. 20402. Much quicker, if you have MasterCard, Visa, or Choice, is to call (202) 783-3238 and charge it.

Do what you can and then see about hiring a lawyer or the next best thing, a patent services firm, which is less expensive. Remember what a patent can and cannot do for you. The best way to think about a patent is as a reward, a gift of a monopoly from the government for seventeen years for you and you alone to benefit from your discovery in exchange for your willingness to share it with the world. If Alexander Graham Bell did not know that he would reap the rewards of his invention without fear of being copied, he might never have made that first phone call to Philadelphia in 1875.

To get a patent, you must show that you have invented or discovered an art, a machine, or a manufacturing process, or an improvement to an existing product, that is both new and useful.

If and when you decide to hire a lawyer, shop around. Many people are reluctant to do this, afraid that the lawyers will feel like any other commodity subject to comparison shopping. A good lawyer respects a client who looks around and compares credentials and track records. And lawyers give more attention and better service to clients they feel are smart enough to differentiate.

If you are lucky enough to have an attorney as part of your domestic scene, by all means consult him. There's nothing like a lawyer on family retainer to give you advice. Be suspicious, however, if he gives you only one name and the chap just happens to have been a fraternity brother.

Notice I don't suggest that you actually use the family lawyer. A generalist who handles trusts, estates, family investments, property, etc., is not what you need. You need a specialist in one specific area. You don't want a lawyer who isn't doing patents every waking second of his working life trying to get a patent for you. The generalist would be learning about patent law on your nickel. A patent attorney is ready to go, already up to speed on what you need. There will be no wasted motion.

The best way to find an expert is by word-of-mouth and then following up by calls to the local bar association, consulting *Martindale-Hubbell Law Directory* (in large libraries; it gives biographical information on almost every practicing lawyer in the United States), and former and current clients. When you have narrowed your list down to three or four, call for a consultation, a quarter-hour meeting (usually not billed), in which you discuss your needs and establish (or don't establish) some rapport. You also should discuss money.

You should not rule out legal clinics, like Hyatt and others. Although some clinics concentrate solely on wills, estates, divorce, personal bankruptcy, and real estate, many legal clinics now take on routine business matters.

In addition to legal clinics, there are nonlaw firms that handle patent and trademark applications. These firms often employ lawyers but charge less because nonlawyers do the bulk of the work. Some of these firms, located in the same office complex as the U.S. Office of Patents and Trademarks in suburban Virginia, are practically part of the patent office, since they do so much work there. Because of the high volume and the specialization, you will generally pay a lot less than if you go to a law firm. Every large city has these specialized nonlaw firms— Washington, D.C., has twelve. You will find them listed under "Patent Searches" in the Yellow Pages.

As to money, under no circumstances should you—a small entrepreneur—consider paying a retainer. A retainer is a monthly fee against which hours actually used are billed. By paying a retainer, you ensure that a particular lawyer will be available when you need him. Lawyers are almost always available when you need them. You cannot afford a retainer. You want to be billed at an hourly rate for hours used, with ten to thirty days to pay. That's it. Most lawyers will recognize the difference between you as a client and General Motors and not insist on the up-front money. The possibility of working on a contingent-fee basis—where the lawyer works for less per hour in exchange for a percentage of the final take—is not likely to come up. Contingency fees are generally reserved for litigated cases, such as personal injury, where the potential for a large damage award is present.

One of the best ways to make sure you aren't overcharged or sloppily billed is to keep track of every time you talk to your lawyer (they do charge for phone calls, so don't chat), to find out the minimum chunk of time they bill for (you may talk six minutes but the firm bills in quarter-hour chunks), and to insist on an itemized bill. A lump-sum bill "$750 for services rendered" is totally out of line.

You should not do business with a firm whose minimum billable unit is a quarter hour—that's just too much. Reasonable firms use the tenth-of-an-hour unit—every six minutes—which keeps the tab down.

And keep these things in mind:

- Don't sign a retainer agreement without reading it carefully. You practically need an attorney to vet your agreement with an attorney. Look out for the "earned retainer," a particularly virulent strain of retainer. That's money up front that the lawyer gets from you for the privilege of doing business with him. He doesn't bill against it. It's a sunk cost and ridiculous. Walk out the door.

- Agree to pay costs incurred on your behalf only if they are cleared with you first. If your lawyer thinks a $100 lunch would be just the thing to soften up a distributor, you should get a chance to say no, or have the lunch yourself.

- If you see prorated charges for overhead, head elsewhere. Lawyers charge enough already without adding a percentage of heat and light costs. Some have the nerve to charge you for secretarial time, photocopying, and the janitor who swabs down the executive toilet. Forget it.

- Ask for a sample bill. If the lawyer won't show you one, again walk out. The bill speaks volumes. It's the only way to tell how that retainer agreement really works in practice. The bill should be very specific, listing the date the service was rendered, what it was (telephone call to patent office, preparation of application), time spent on each, and what that comes to in cold, hard cash. If there were any costs (filing fees, transcripts, record searches), these should be described and have been approved in advance. You can also see if there are any catchall categories where charges for overhead and other things are hidden.

- In general, don't go for a flat fee. A patent can take a few hours. It can take several weeks. You just don't know. But you can bet that the flat fee offered is going to protect the lawyer in the event it takes several weeks.

Whether you choose a large law firm, a sole practitioner, a legal clinic, or a patent services corporation, do not be afraid to discuss fees up front. I'm amazed at how certain professions have managed to create an atmosphere where the discussion of money is taboo, as if what they do is so sacred that it would be tawdry to suggest that they could charge less than the moon and the stars for it. The law is not an art, it's not a science, it's a service. Negotiate accordingly.

# Eleven

# Getting It Made

If the thought of having your product made in Hong Kong scares you, it should. It probably will cost more to get it made in the United States, but remember that old saw: There's no place like home.

Now that you've got some orders, you have a big decision to make: How in the world do you get these things made?

In this case, I am going to tell you to do as I say, not as I did. I really didn't have to decide about where the best place to manufacture Wallwalkers would be. Wallwalkers were already being manufactured in Japan. The best thing for me to do, I decided, was to continue to do what was working. Although Japan is a fiercely expensive country to use, for me using it was a virtually risk-free way of conducting business. If I had gone to another country, I might have saved on manufacturing costs but also ended up with shipments of Wallwalkers that didn't stick to the walls or were the wrong color or fell apart. They might have arrived late, after the fad had expired, or not at all.

Generally speaking, it is a lot easier and there are fewer headaches if you deal with a manufacturer in the United States rather than abroad. In the United States you have far more control over everything that is going on. You can see what is occurring more easily if your factory is in a nearby town or even across the country than if your manufacturer is located halfway around the world. And *seeing is believing*. You don't want to be relying on some guy telling you those widgets are flying off the assembly line at a hundred per hour when, in fact, the whole plant staff is off observing some obscure religious holiday. Knowing there is a problem is the first step. Doing something about it is another. You need to be able to get to your plant short of crossing several time zones.

There are other advantages to manufacturing in the United States. You get better control over the kinds of raw materials and ingredients used in your product. Quality control is easier because you can see how clean or how dirty the factory is and whether the guy screwing in butterfly nuts is nodding off at every third widget.

It is more expensive to manufacture here, in large part because labor costs are so high. But when you start out, your volume will be low and you don't really save money by manufacturing abroad until you are turning out high volume. In any event, you can always start out manufacturing here. If your item takes off, there is nothing to stop you from then moving abroad.

There are inexpensive ways to manufacture here. This country is filled with small, independent manufacturing companies that can do only *small* jobs. Personal attention and quick turnaround time are the selling points of these operations and they are perfect for running off several crates of widgets.

Some of the best small manufacturing operations in the United States are run by handicapped people. These organizations exist in many communities. For information you can call Goodwill Industries, the Lighthouse, or similar organizations listed in the Yellow Pages under either "Charitable Organizations" or "Social Service Organizations." These groups are set up to do assembly-type work at very reasonable prices, and minimum orders are very small. They are particularly good at packaging.

When your volume increases or if you need a huge rush order (it is hard to accomplish the latter with a small manufacturer here; also, the overtime labor would kill you), look into manufacturing abroad. But do not undertake this on your own unless you have special ties to the country you are considering. The brother-in-law of your college roommate with a fellowship at Peking University does not count. You need someone with experience handling overseas suppliers, someone who speaks the language, knows the culture, is expert at quality control, and has dealt with customs officials. This could be someone established inside the country, or an importer who deals with a number of manufacturers within a given country.

A good way to get started if you have no leads is to contact the embassy of the country you are interested in doing business with. Call the embassy office in Washington, D.C., or one of its consulates in a major city across the country. Each office has a commercial attaché whose job is to attract business. They will be very helpful.

In deciding which country offers the best deal, don't forget to calculate import duties, a considerable cost that varies wildly from country to country. Duties on the Wallwalker added about 12 percent to the cost. A product that may be duty-free coming in from Korea may have a 10 percent duty added if it comes in from Hong Kong. And duties are not a constant. An item that was duty-free last month may carry one this month. And one that was 5 percent last year might be 10 percent this year.

I eventually moved production away from Japan. The impetus was the premium deal with Kellogg. The first consideration was that Kellogg was placing the Wallwalker in a food product—cereal—so that it had to meet a different set of specifications. The second consideration was price. I had to get my cost down because as a premium item the Wallwalker would command a far smaller profit. My first thought was to manufacture in the United States. That turned out to be prohibitively expensive—not so much because of the manufacturing itself but because of the labor costs associated with packaging. My item was one of the few that has to be packaged by human hands because it is so sticky. The Lighthouse wouldn't have been able to handle the volume. Then I started looking into Taiwan and Korea, which appeared to have the best prices. I eliminated Taiwan because it is the knockoff capital of the world. I thought it would be impossible to operate confidentially there. Place an order for a hundred thousand at one factory, and ten other factories would be pumping out knockoffs before the first real Wallwalker hit the wall. At that point I decided on Korea. I still had to spend a lot of time in that country. The factory itself had to exceed the standards of any other there. You have to be able to eat off the floor, since Wallwalkers were going to be in the same box as that All-American foodstuff corn flakes.

There is a middle ground for those who want the economy of the Far East but the certainty of their own backyard. Most products require a mold—the original from which all the others are made. You may need only one (the Wallwalker took thirty-five before it was over), but the mold is the most expensive part of the process. For example, if a mold costs $30,000 to make in Ohio, it probably will cost $10,000 in Korea. Most of the reasons for not manufacturing abroad can be overlooked here. Having the mold made abroad is a one-shot deal. It's not like having a factory to oversee. And then you can produce here, getting the best of both worlds.

One more caveat about manufacturing abroad: In the age of the fluctuating dollar, it is hard to calculate what your product is going to cost in the end. The cost of your labor is going to change in, say, Japan as the yen rises against the dollar. The same goes for the cost of your raw material. There are a lot of risks you have to take. Think long and hard before you make currency futures one of them. Leave that to Ivan Boesky.

# Twelve

# The Price Is Right

> *Be a little greedy. You're giving something terrific to the world, and the world will be happy to pay for it. Don't sell yourself short.*

You can do everything else right in launching your fad. You can get plastered all over the front page of the local paper and get two minutes on all three networks. You can sell millions of your widgets. But if you didn't price it right, you won't make a dime.

Nothing in fad marketing is as important as pricing it right. The price you decide on when you first put your fad on the market is the one you'll be working from for its entire life-span. You can never go higher than your starting price. And if your starting price isn't high enough, your margin will be down to zero before you know it. That's because as your product gets lower on the retail chain, so does your price. What sells at Bloomingdale's at the start of a fad's run for $3.00 is going to be $1.79 at K mart a few months later.

One of the biggest mistakes people make in figuring out the price at the start is calculating the cost down to the last hundredth of a cent. First of all, this is an impossible task. Second, beginners can never contemplate all the variables involved and so err miserably anyway. Besides, what it costs you to make an item is only one factor in deciding what price to charge and is by no means determinative. Calculating the cost of the plastic and rubber and other raw materials is not hard. It's the peripherals that are going to be tough, and unless you have a "planning division," you won't know how to deal with them. For instance, you may start out marketing on the East Coast. Then you get a lot of publicity and see a nationwide market. Once you are selling on the West Coast, transportation becomes a large element in your costs—one you never factored in.

Beginners often get around the problem of figuring out what to charge by calculating the cost of making the item and then tacking on, say, 50 percent to be safe. This, they figure, will cover everything. Well, maybe, maybe not. This is why you shouldn't be afraid of overcharging. On the contrary, charge as much as you think you can get because you're going to need that safety net.

At first, 50 percent might seem like a lot, but often it's not enough to cover the cost of delivery, the cost of collecting the money, the cost of the deadbeats, the cost of promotion. Give yourself a 50 percent margin and you are giving yourself a huge headache, a disaster waiting to happen.

Let's break down what that widget really costs. First of all, you have to figure distribution is going to cost you between 7 and 20 percent. This comes out of your 50 percent margin. Then there always are some people who aren't going to pay you, so figure 5 cents there. Very often you are going to have to deliver the widget free, so you have to allow another 5 percent there. Even if you don't advertise at all, you still have to get out and promote the thing. And even if you stay in your own area, you have to factor in gasoline and oil, so figure another 5 cents. Then you have mailing and phoning costs. In fads, you always need a lot of Federal Express—remember Fad Standard Time. Tack on 10 cents. So if you price that widget at $1.50, you are paying people to take it off your hands.

I'm always shocked at how low fad people price themselves. Fads are supposed to be cheap, true. But they're not giveaways. Fad people are so happy that anybody wants to buy this crazy gadget they have been carrying around in their heads for years that they want to write a thank-you note to every purchaser.

Fad people dream big but think small. If you make a thousand units of a widget at $1.00 and sell it for $1.50, you think, "Gee, I'm making $500 on this." While that might work at a thousand units when your costs are minimal, it's going to kill you at fifty thousand units. A thousand units and you are dealing with a few stores in a small area; at fifty thousand you're in the big leagues, with all that implies: transportation costs, sales commissions, returns, collection problems, and paperwork that can sink you.

I come at pricing from the other direction. I calculate all my costs—variable and otherwise—and tuck that figure away into a corner of my brain and temporarily forget it. If you're constantly worrying about every cent of what it costs you to make it, you don't have a fad item. Conventional marketing rules don't apply. You aren't Procter & Gamble trying to push yet another brand of detergent in a highly competitive market where the right price point is vital. What you are selling is unique, so you have a lot more leeway in determining a price. A fad is a notion, a piece of fun. It is worth what you say it's worth.

The law of supply and demand operates to some extent in fads. When it's hot, you can't get a sufficient number out there fast enough to meet demand. That means the market will support a huge margin—say, a 300 percent markup. About the time you can get production up to meet demand, demand is leveling off—remember, fads burn out. Then the knockoffs have had time to kick in and are flooding the market, creating an excess of supply. So inevitably the price drops.

Here is how knockoffs ruin your price. Say there are five factories in Taiwan turning out widgets that you had been buying for 50 cents and selling for $1.25 when the fad was hot and you were the only conduit. Now there are thirty importers bringing them into the United States and three thousand retailers ready to buy. The first ten importers go to K mart and undercut your price of $1.25 by offering the widget for 75 cents. Then the next ten importers hear about this and are willing to go down to 60 cents. The other importers panic and go to the chains and say they will sell them for 50 cents apiece. Now they are down to selling it at manufacturing cost. They are losing money at 50 cents. But at this point they just want to unload. Then the other importers panic even more because they envision not being able to sell theirs at any price. They "drop their pants," as the industry puts it, and come in at 40 cents, just hoping not to get stuck with a crateful of widgets. Now your fad is in free fall. The importers have butchered each other. You are saved from getting slaughtered only if you started high enough when the fad was hot and supply was under your control.

You have to ask yourself a second question: "Am I going to sell a lot of units very cheaply at the chain level, or a few units very high at the boutique level?" Two things come in to play here.

First, how long will it take to establish your item as a trendy one by selling at boutiques where you can command top dollar? A stint at the Bloomingdale's level is great if you can get it, even if it has to be cut very short. This is because the salespeople at Bloomingdale's are trained to show people what to do with a Wallwalker. They make it trendy for you. This won't happen if you start out at K mart. Second, how long a life do you realistically think the thing has? If you stay too long at the boutiques, someone is going to beat you to the chains. If the life is very short, you have to drop the boutiques right away and go for volume at the chains. Keep in mind that Bloomingdale's doesn't want it after it's been at K mart.

While you are making your image at the boutique level, you are also making a lot of money per unit. The item you will sell for $5.00 at K mart you can sell for $10 at a boutique.

This is where your delicate sense of timing must come into play. That $10 price tag is making the knockoff artists salivate. They look at that and see a $4 wholesale margin to play with. Lick ing their chops, they have sent one of your widgets to Taiwan, and three weeks later they are importing those babies at a rapid clip.

That doesn't mean you shouldn't do it. It will take the knockoffs a while, and in the meantime you are selling as many as you can get at $10, clearing $4. So if you sell a hundred thousand units at $10 in, say, three weeks when you have the market to yourself, you are going to do just as well as selling two hundred thousand at $5.00—a higher volume stretched out over a much longer period. Remember, you are always fighting the clock.

You can take the opposite track: price your

widget to retail for $3.00 from the start and hope to keep out the knockoffs altogether. They look at the widget and say with a sniff, "A fifty-cent margin. Not worth it." But you have made a sacrifice to do this. You have given up the huge markup you can get at the start of your fad. And the sacrifice doesn't always work. If an item is hot enough some of the potential knockoffs are going to say, "A fifty-cent margin. Half a million units. What the heck?"

The timing on when you move from the $10 boutique to the cut-price chain is going to vary somewhat with every fad. With Wallwalkers I planned to move to the chains when I saw the fad peaking. But as it turned out, I couldn't wait that long. I had to drop the boutiques and the high markup before I wanted to because of the piece on the *CBS Evening News* on December 27, 1982. It turns out that the piece ran in the Far East, and the factories were humming with the sound of fake wallwalkers rolling down the conveyor belt before Dan Rather signed off. Wallwalkers hadn't peaked yet—I had sold only twenty-five thousand— but I decided to sell to the chains anyway. Within two weeks of the CBS News piece, I had orders for seventeen million Wallwalkers. And since at that time I could get only two hundred thousand Wallwalkers made a week, I couldn't do both the boutiques and the chains.

Another factor you have to consider in pricing is that fads—the most profitable ones, anyway— are impulse items. Impulse items have to be low-priced. If you can't decide to buy it in the amount of time you stand in the express check-out line, it costs too much to be a mass-market fad.

Impulse-item price levels go up with inflation, so you fad people still make the mistake of going too low. Impulse is no longer below $1.00. Impulse buying has crept up. Retailers don't want to carry a 99-cent item anymore. It's not worth the trouble it takes to ring it up, even if they sell a thousand. It won't get shelf space, it won't get any display; it won't be restocked, even.

People, ordinary customers, have an innate sense of what something should cost. Get a bunch of your friends together and get them to write down on a piece of paper what they would pay for something. You would be surprised at how close the prices are.

At my last Fad Fair, a couple from Michigan had a great item—a shower poster for children. It was made of plastic and designed to stick to the shower wall with water. It looked great and attracted a lot of attention at the fair. But the couple was pricing the poster at $2.50 retail. Ridiculous. I took one look at it and said, "This is an $8.99 item." I had several other people tell me what they would pay for this item. They all hovered in the $10 range. I asked the couple why they priced the poster so low, and they said because it cost only 80 cents to make. Ignore that. It's interesting, a starting point, but it has less to do with the price you choose than with what people perceive the product to be worth. Paper posters sell for more than $2.50, and this had a lot of novelty.

The guy who came to Fad Fair and ended up on the *Tonight Show* made the mistake of pricing his Ladyfinger too low. He started out with it at 97 cents retail. He left himself no margin at all. All he could do was go down from there. He could have easily priced it at $1.49 or $1.99. It would still have been snapped up at the cash register.

What I did in pricing the Wallwalker was a

combination of the above. Initially I thought of pricing the Wallwalker all the way from $9.99 on down to 99 cents. I like nines. I knew instinctively not to price it at what it cost, plus my variable costs. My cost was about 25 cents to manufacture the thing, plus a 12.3 percent import duty. If you figure in some overhead and distribution costs, I estimated that the unit cost of my item was about 60 cents.

In the end I sold my product for $1.25 wholesale, which meant it sold for $2.50 retail initially. If anything, I could have priced it higher. Lower, and the knockoffs would have come in anyway. If you misjudge the market and come in low and you make a little bit of money and it dies, you should have gone high. But if it is something like the Frisbee, that is just going to keep going on for years, you are smart to come in low, and give yourself a fighting chance of keeping the market to yourself.

Most items start high and work their way lower. This phenomenon is not to be confused with the pricing of something like the VCR or the Cuisinart, not true fads, whose price comes down as the technology improves. The VCR started at $3,000 and now is sold as low as $200. The Cuisinart started at $300 or so and now can be bought for close to $100.

Some fads never get a chance to drop their price. It goes to zero because the market disappears. Take Laser Tag. Hot for six months, it sold for about $50. The fad dropped off so precipitously after those six months that Laser Tag had a hard time finding buyers at $20.

The Swatch is an exception, a fad that has managed to hold on and, so, to hold on to its price. Part of that is due to its tightly controlled distribution. Swatch doesn't want to be a mass-merchandise product. It doesn't want to sell at K mart. That could hurt the image they have decided to go with—a high-end fashion statement. So as long as Swatch lasts, its price lasts. I could have kept my price for the Wallwalker at $2.50 if I had not wanted to go to the nationwide chains, which meant $1.79.

I had a decent margin even when K mart dropped the thing to $1.79. This gave me the margin I needed to pay the high percent commission you have to pay to get the top distributors. I still ended up making an average of between 30 and 50 cents per item.

At the boutique level I sold a couple of hundred thousand at $2.50 retail. Then I sold millions at the K mart level. At the start of the mass-market level, I was still making a huge margin because our publicity was so excellent I didn't need to drop my price.

I kept my price to the K marts of the world at $1.25 and was able to give people a 5 percent discount or a 5 percent cooperative advertising allowance, which is normal operating procedure. It was amazing that we were able to sell the one-million-unit orders at the same price as the three-thousand-unit orders, but you, too, can do that at the peak of your fad. In the end, I sold 200 million Wallwalkers.

Still, at $2.50 we got knocked off like crazy. I knew we would. It isn't the guys who do the knocking off who make the money, it's the retailers. This is how it goes: The knockoffs eat each other up by underselling each other. The importers don't make any money because their margin is small to begin with. Retailers buy the knockoffs for 60 cents and sell them for $2.50, just the way they buy mine for $1.25 and sell them for $2.50. Eventually the knockoffs ruin the market for everybody.

# Thirteen

# Guerrilla Advertising: Grabbing Hold of the Media Monster and Making It Work for You

> *The easiest decision you will ever have to make is about the type of advertising campaign you should launch, since you won't be launching any advertising campaign at all.*

One of the great things about being in the fad business is that it's the only one where you get more attention if you're an amateur. In the early days of the Wallwalker, before I had made any big distribution deals, I asked a good friend in Washington, D.C., whose family owned a large drugstore chain with a big toy section what I should do next.

Wanting to help, my friend introduced me to his toy buyer, who'd been in the business for twenty years and had great contacts. The toy buyer put me on to a big toy executive in New York. The toy mogul took a look at the Wallwalker, sniffed, and said, "You're gonna get killed."

He said amateurs had no place in the toy business. An amateur like me would get completely wiped out. His analysis was "two weeks tops," and then it would die overnight. Not only that, he had seen the toy before and didn't think much of it. That was pretty discouraging.

I could have given up right then, but I decided to stick with my own instincts. Just because he had been in the toy business longer than I'd been alive was no reason to quit.

Besides, being an amateur was my ace in the

hole. If I hadn't been an amateur, I would never have captured the imagination of the media. The little guy with a dream who makes a million is a lot more newsworthy than Mattel making money from some children's television program tie-in such as Captain Power.

Being newsworthy is the name of the game when you're trying to market a fad. You will need free publicity, the only sort you can afford. Maybe Mattel can throw $20 million into an advertising campaign to promote a new toy, but you can't do that. A national advertising campaign costs $1 million, minimum. (A single thirty-second spot on *Miami Vice* will set you back $250,000.) You don't have $1 million, so not launching an ad campaign is an easy decision. Some people think it's worth doing a third-rate $200,000 campaign. That's because they're stuck on another of those old clichés I told you to put out of your mind: It pays to advertise.

Take the case of the advertising man with no money to advertise. Gary Dahl had toiled for fifteen years as a copywriter and commercial art-ist at an ad agency when he quit his job and started to sell rocks, millions of them. With no capital to promote his creation, the Pet Rock, he set out with a bunch of homemade news releases and some photos of himself surrounded by boxes of the Rocks. He dropped one off at *Newsweek*'s San Francisco office. The magazine picked up on it, sent a reporter and photographer to Dahl's hometown, Los Gatos, California, and did a half-page story on him and his Pet Rock. This was the break he needed. After the *Newsweek* story he got tons of free publicity, hundreds of interviews, and found himself on the *Tonight Show*—twice. The Pet Rock became one of the most successful gift items ever, with sales averaging a hundred thousand a day at the height of the craze. In just three months, sales amounted to over $4 million. And all because Dahl couldn't afford advertising.

Knerr and Melin also didn't have an advertising budget for the Hula-Hoop or the Frisbee. That's why they gave the Hula-Hoop to kids, who were picked up on local TV using the thing because it made such an amusing sight. With the Frisbee, they sponsored contests, also a natural television story. They started small—with giveaways in parks, to recreational departments, on college campuses, and at beaches—building enough interest to make the tournaments media events. Of course, the toy itself is a natural, lofting fifty or sixty feet into the air and then coming down far enough to be caught with one hand—but only if that hand had taken into consideration the trajectory into which the Frisbee was thrown. It was a toy that took energy and skill, perfect for the local sports reporters looking for an offbeat story. Eventually a hundred million were sold.

My story is similar. People think I'm some sort of public-relations genius; others think I'm just incredibly lucky. But you can bet I was prepared when the opportunities came along. There are several ways to capitalize on opportunity and there are several ways to create the opportunities so you'll have something to capitalize on. No two stories are ever exactly the same, but you can use what I did as a blueprint for getting yourself in the public eye.

Because I'd already seen how effective personal demonstrations were in selling the Wallwalker, I wanted to demonstrate it personally for the entire country and Canada, and I wanted to do it in a week, before the fad died out. I needed a story in a national newspaper. I was fortunate that the *Washington Post*, if not a national newspaper, has national distribution. It also happens to be my hometown newspaper.

Two months after my initial discovery I filled a backpack with Wallwalkers and canvassed as many small shops in the downtown D.C. area as I could. Many of them fell within walking distance of the *Washington Post*. I concentrated on the coffee shops, newsstands, delis, and drugstores around the newspaper's offices. Before too long a Wallwalker caught the eye of Nina Hyde, the *Washington Post* fashion editor whom I think of as the godmother of the Wallwalker, who wrote a Style Section piece on how it was going to be a big fad.

Later the Business Section of the *Washington Post* picked up the story.

Years later I met Ben Bradlee, the *Washington Post* editor who broke the Watergate story. I told him that the *Post* had changed my life. He looked at me nervously and asked how. I think he was happy to find out that the *Post* does change the lives of some people for the better. The trick is to be on the front page of the Style or Business Section, not Section A, where everyone is getting indicted.

It took just under eleven weeks from the time the package for my kids arrived in October 1982 and the first article in the *Post*. This was fast. The timing was excellent in that the article appeared just before Christmas.

It will make it easier for you in trying to get media attention and not feel like a fool while doing it if you keep in mind that reporters need you almost as much as you need them. You might easily lose sight of that because usually there are many more stories than there are minutes on the evening news. But reporters find themselves looking for stories they can turn to on slow news days, of which there are more than you might think. All weekends are slow news days, except when an accident occurs. August always is slow, which is why you see so many dog-days-of-August stories. Ditto holidays.

I got on the *CBS Evening News* because it was a weekend when nothing happened. Jim Bakker was not having sex, there were no ten-car pileups on the San Bernardino Freeway, no home run records were broken, and no famous celebrity died. A producer at CBS came up with the idea of doing a piece on Wallwalkers when he saw how intensely reporters and cameramen in the Washington bureau were playing with Wallwalkers, throwing them on TV monitors, and watching them slowly walk down. On one of those slow news days I was telling you about, a cameraman caught one of the Wallwalkers doing his thing and beamed it to New York. A producer yelled, "Get me Bruce Morton!" And the next thing I knew I was being interviewed for a spot on the *CBS Evening News* and Dan Rather was saying at the end, "I'll take a dozen."

Newspaper articles multiply like rabbits. If an article runs in one paper, you can be sure others will pick up on it. The calls will come to you. It's as if that first article legitimizes you as a bona fide news event, and no one else has to make a news judgment, they just have to get you on the line and get the interview.

A news story has tremendous impact on buyers. One newspaper clip is worth a thousand paid advertisements when it comes to sales. Bloomingdale's considers one clip equal to a full-page ad in *The*

*New York Times* when placing an order and assigning display space.

Some people think that a glossy press kit is how you get the attention of the media, but if you'd ever worked for a paper, magazine, or TV station you would know how many elegant-looking, four-color press kits come through the door. They get promptly filed in the wastebasket with no more than a passing glance.

A woman who writes for *Time* magazine told me that the Lifestyle section of *Time* gets over two thousand press releases on new ideas every week. Most of them never get opened.

If you can't give up the press kit idea, at least make it amateur. Use colorful Magic Markers and a snapshot taken with a Polaroid. It's more likely to command attention than a cheap imitation of a glossy brochure. Those just end up looking like Communist propaganda.

Fortunately, I was in Washington, and all the major news bureaus and news wires have offices there. If I'd been in Wyoming, obviously, it would have been more difficult. You could argue that Washington isn't that great compared to New York or Los Angeles, which are trendy, which Washington with all its bureaucrats and lawyers is not.

In L.A. or New York, on the other hand, there are so many weird things going on all the time that it is hard to get anybody's attention. Throwing a rubber octopus on the wall in a restaurant at Hollywood and Vine would be considered normal behavior unworthy of much more than a passing glance. In New York, Dan Rather has to avoid not being overrun by craziness just walking to his office.

But in the nation's capital, you have to do some hard looking to come up with anything offbeat.

It's a pretty serious crowd, talking about SALT II and the deficit all the time. What passes for an offbeat story is George Shultz wearing a yellow tie with his gray flannel suit. So you can get attention much more easily. That is why the *Washington Post* did a full-fledged feature very early on the Wallwalker.

Wherever you are, if things really start flying on TV and in the newspapers, you have to try to pace the stories so the publicity suits your time-table and not the other way around. You want the stories to run when your Wallwalker orders are hitting the stores, not before, and you don't want to oversaturate, although that's not usually the problem.

Not being overly anxious also makes you more desirable. Reporters are always suspicious of people who seek them out and are more likely to suspend disbelief entirely when they seek some-one out. They are grateful when the latter group responds to their incisive, in-depth questions. At the height of Wallwalkers, there was plenty of interest, and I responded.

When the press is receptive, accept all the in-terviews that are offered and don't play favorites. Give as much time and energy to a reporter from the *Cedar Rapids Gazette* as you would one from the *Los Angeles Times*. This is because editors in big cities often pick up ideas from smaller papers, and because distributors and store managers don't discriminate among clips as much as you might think. They look for breadth.

Television is a bit different. Even distributors know the difference between a spot on the na-tional network news and the local. Within a day after I appeared on the *CBS Evening News* with Dan Rather, I had twelve hundred calls, a lot of them from other reporters wanting to do interviews. The amount of other stories and buyers that piece generated is incalculable. I still haven't returned all those calls.

It is very hard to get the attention of the network talk and interview shows. I got on a lot of them but never made it to the *Tonight Show*. I did everything, including throwing Wallwalkers on the wall at Morton's, a fashionable restaurant in Los Angeles where Johnny Carson was eating, but I only succeeded in making a fool of myself.

But making a fool of myself paid off later. At Spago, a restaurant in Los Angeles favored by media people, I threw some Wallwalkers onto a mirror. Eating nearby were some NBC television executives who, unlike Carson, thought it was funny. They already knew about the Wallwalker, of course—by this time it was a fad that had been around for about four months. But this made them think of television possibilities. About ten months later, in December 1983, I had a Christmas prime-time special on NBC starring the Wallwalkers as cartoon characters.

That same trip to Los Angeles yielded a call from the executive vice-president at MGM/United Artists in May 1983. He wanted to use Wallwalkers to promote the new James Bond movie *Octopussy*. He said that if he had known about Wallwalkers sooner, he would have used them in the movie. The filming in London had already concluded, but he told me that if I could make Wallwalkers that were about three or four feet in diameter, he would have Roger Moore, who had starred in the film, throw them against the World Trade Center in New York from a helicopter.

This is not a very original idea. Many people get publicity with the World Trade Center, although they risk getting arrested at the end. I don't know how Roger Moore felt about landing on a police blotter somewhere, but I wouldn't have minded a few hours in the clinker for my Wallwalker. But the Port Authority told us that tremendous wind around the Trade Center made it impossible to throw anything from a helicopter. A Wallwalker thrown against the Trade Center and picked up by a big gust of wind could carry across the river to Brooklyn, where it would hit some lady on the head and they would be sued. Their insurance policy does not cover such incidents. So they didn't let us do it. Instead, MGM bought tens of thousands of Wallwalkers to give out at their world premiere of the movie. It went very well. One day I got a call from a collector of James Bond memorabilia. He was at a spy convention in New York and he told me that the hottest new item there was the new James Bond Wacky Wallwalker. I said, "What is that?" Apparently MGM attached their own label with the "007" logo to my Wallwalkers and called it the *Octopussy* Wallwalker. There were only ten thousand of them made, and they were in great demand. MGM hired women to dress in harem outfits to go all around Manhattan, Los Angeles, and Chicago throwing Wallwalkers all over the place. This was the sexiest my Wallwalker ever got.

# Fourteen

# Getting It on the Shelf: The Right Distributor for You

> *Distribution is a great sport for sharks. To quote Satchel Paige, "Look back, someone may be gaining on you."*

Finding the right distributor is one of the most important parts of making your fad successful. But it is one of the parts over which you have the least control. That's because there is no one right distributor. There are distributors, called "bullets" in the trade, who are particularly good with certain accounts and can be found only by word of mouth.

Forget about looking for some magic list of good distributors broken down by type of product or territory or whatever. Such a list simply doesn't exist. The list of buyers and distributors in Appendix 3 is far more useful.

Distributors will come to you when you have built sufficient demand for your product. The distributor cannot go around creating a demand for your fad. It would be great if he could. But his job is to go around satisfying demand that, for the most part, is already there.

The mistake most fadsters make is to contact distributors too early. What's a distributor going to do when an inventor from Ohio comes to him and shows him a prototype of his new windup toy? He is going to ask, "How many have you sold at boutiques? Where have you been written up? What TV programs have you been on? Where are your ads?" Then he is going to say, "Get outta here with your silly windup toy. Don't waste my time." You aren't ready for a distributor until you can give him the necessary ammunition—news clips—that he can take to chain store and other buyers and say, "Here's proof that these items are hot. You'd be smart to order a thousand dozen."

It's a little like going to the voice coach at Juilliard before your voice is ready. The coach could teach you everything she knows, but if your voice isn't mature or you haven't practiced your scales enough, her vast knowledge is lost on you.

The same with going to a distributor before your factory is geared up and ready to produce however many he gets orders for.

If you hope to go straight into the bigger stores, in particular the chains, you may fall into the "test marketing trap." The chains don't want to take the risk on national distribution because your fad isn't far enough along, so they will try to get you to give them your product for a trial. "Give me a hundred dozen and we will test-market it in our stores in Detroit." This is death to your fad. You will never survive, even if you get an A+ and all hundred dozen sell out in the first day. This is because no single product is important to a big chain and a fad doesn't last long enough for the results of a test market to work its way back up the decision ladder. A hundred dozen of a product just falls off the computer. No fad can survive test marketing—not the Hula-Hoop, not the Frisbee, not the Wallwalker.

Rather than wasting time searching out and trying to get appointments with hotshot distributors, or being reduced to a "test marketing," face up to the fact that at the beginning you have to be your own distributor, along with being your own packager, your own accountant, your own collection agency, and your own promoter.

When people complain to me about not having anyone to sell their product, I tell them, "Who has a sales force when you start out? Who wants a sales force when you start out? It's just another group of expensive people to worry about."

At the beginning when I was importing several thousand Wallwalkers at a time, I was the packager, the promoter, the sales force, the distributor. That's how it has to be. You don't need a license, you don't need training, you just need a belief in the product and a lot of energy to get out there and sell it.

This isn't going to work when your product takes off. But this is one way to make it big. You serve as your own distributor to the trendy gift-shop-boutique-type places. Trendsetters shop in these places, maybe a news reporter or two. You are looking for your big break, which in this day and age is often a media break and, in the meantime, you are building a groundswell of demand for your product to create that break. You are not wasting time trying to get an appointment with the distributor who has a straight line to the buyer for Wal-Mart.

I got my big media break by being my own distributor and PR man, as I told you before, and then I had distributors knocking down my door. After the big spot on the *CBS Evening News,* I had them camping in my backyard. I had phone messages stacked to the ceiling. That was good because by this time I needed distributors, and so will you. You can't go to all the chains yourself and keep the boutiques where you started out happy. It s not possible.

The good distributors have their ears to the ground so that when a product comes along that's hot they can jump on it. They listen mostly to the media, but they also stay in touch with their accounts who will say to them, "I keep hearing about this thing called a Wacky Wallwalker. Why don't you get me some." So they will come in search of you when the time is right. Then it is up to you to choose among them.

Now that you have all these distributors champing at the bit, how do you know which one to choose? It's just common sense. That's all there is. They will give you references, but if your fad is hot, you are not going to have time to check. For starters you can distinguish between those distributors who are going to work well with the chains and the ones who are just right for the mom-and-pop stores, and you can find out which ones have the best relationship with each individual chain, but you can't do much more.

All distribution used to be territorial. It was a feudal system where one guy had Chicago and no one messed with him, and another guy had Detroit. Then you might have someone who had the Southeast. This system is of no relevance today. Just forget it, because the world is divided into chains and into small independents.

Let's say you give Illinois and Indiana to this distributor operating out of Chicago. He knows the shopping center shops and the newsstand on the corner and places like that. Fine. But Sears' headquarters is in Chicago and, if you don't know any better, this guy is going to try to get you to give him Sears as well. Don't fall for it. The guy who does the mom-and-pops in Chicago isn't going to make it past the security guard in the lobby of the Sears Tower.

You can't give the guy in Chicago Sears just because the guy's in Chicago. The guy who has his talons into the national buyer for Sears may be sitting in Miami.

So how do you find him? (See Appendix 3 for a list of distributors and buyers at all the major chains.) The best and quickest way is to call Sears and ask who they buy their blankety-blank from. If you've got a piece of hardware, you call the hardware buyer; a toy, the toy buyer; and so on. You work backward here. It's not only the best way to go, it's also the fastest. They are happy to tell you. It's no skin off their backs. It makes their job easier in the end because they don't like a bunch of guys they don't know in shiny suits cluttering up their reception area. Often there is one distributor the guy in hardware buys most of his gadgets from. Great. Even if he gives you a couple of distributors Sears deals with, you have narrowed the universe, and probably any one can do the job for you. Then you get to do a bit of negotiating for the best deal among them.

This is a lot better than coming at it from the other end. Ask a distributor in the Midwest to tell you the name of the best distributor to go to Sears with your product and he will say *I am,* of course. Ask a distributor working Dallas who is the best with the 7-Eleven chain owned by Southland Corporation based in Dallas and he will say himself. After all, I'm here and I know the Dallas business community.

Maybe, maybe not. A lot of factors come into play. For example, let's say that the best distributor to deal with The Southland Corporation in Dallas is sitting in New York and has been doing business with the president of Southland since they both went to graduate school at the University of Chicago. You're lucky if it takes only one phone call to Southland to find that out. You're even luckier if that guy calls you.

Don't believe anyone who says he is a national distributor for fads. There is no such thing. Anyone who tells you that, cross him off your list immediately. There are distributors who are good with certain accounts or types of accounts (see the list of distributors). Some people are good for just one account—say, Thrifty Drug Stores—but that's it. Just give him Thrifty. Don't give him Safeway or anything else. Maybe some other guy is good with one or two of the grocery store chains. You find that most people are good only for one or two accounts because they have worked out a special relationship over the years. Go with it. Don't try to save money by giving the guy who is good with Woolworth's Sears as well.

It is up to you to put together a national distribution team with the distributors you select. You create your own network, and you control it. Get distributors to the ten biggest chains—say, K mart, Woolworth, Sears, Wal-Mart, Thrifty Drug Stores, Revco, Target Stores, Eckhardt Drugs, Toys-"Я"-Us, and Murphy's—and you have national distribution. You will be in about twenty thousand stores.

You also don't want to bother with the guy who does a little bit of business with Sears, who is building up his relationship with Sears. You don't have time for that. You have to go with the guy who already has the relationship. Go with the best, or near-best, even if it means paying up to 20 percent. This is where to put the money you saved by not buying the fancy office equipment and the secretary. A fad could be dead by the time the junior guy just out of Wharton gets his foot in the door. You need a top professional who can go right into the president or at least the merchandise manager for the whole chain and say, "Here is a very hot item. Believe me, I've seen the clips and I believe the maker of these things when he tells me there is a piece about to appear on the Lifestyle page of *Time* magazine. Take five thousand gross—you won't regret it. Go with it and you will be the first chain in the country to have it."

Be careful, too, not to fall for the line of some second-rate distributors who can't cut a major deal with a chain and come to you all excited saying that Wal-Mart has agreed to test-market your product, to take a hundred gross and see how it does in Detroit. See the earlier discussion of test-marketing.

Everything I've said about distributors so far is important. But the most important thing anyone could ever tell you about distributors is that no matter how much a distributor loves you in the beginning, he is going to want to end the affair the second the passion cools.

A few hundred thousands of sales into your fad and a few of your distributors are going to start thinking they are the whole business. They are out there moving the goods, producing all the revenue. "I sell, you don't do anything" is the attitude. You become the guy who had the good fortune and the capital to buy the rights, but that's it.

The second sales lag, this type of distributor will be saying, "I think we should price it differently now," or "Let's make a different size for this store," or "I think we should be giving bigger discounts." No matter how convincing he sounds, the distributor is looking at the business from a very narrow perspective.

At this point you have to keep your broad perspective and nerves of steel. You, as the general of the fad, are on top of the hill with your binoculars, and you know where the artillery is, where the cavalry is, where the trenches are. You can't be swayed by the guy in the field who, because he is down there taking the flak, thinks he knows where the artillery should be.

I had several distributors coming to me about three weeks into the Wallwalker fad, when there were knockoffs underselling us and sales were plateauing, saying, "Drop your pants, Ken. I will only go around selling these things if you drop your price by half. Otherwise it's not worth it to me."

Drop your pants in one market because some distributor is pressuring you and you will have to drop your pants in all of them. You have to get rid of a distributor like that because you can't control him. He will be making deals to make a quick profit and be ruining your market. Think of distributors as sharks. Keep them pointed forward at all times or they will swim around behind you and take a chunk out of your back.

If you aren't the ruthless type, hire someone who is. You need to get rid of the distributors right away who have cooled on your product. If you have kept control of your fad, you can drop a few distributors with no trouble. Go for the second-best distributor for that chain, or take it over yourself. Some of my distributors lost interest when there still was a lot of life left in the Wallwalker. If they had kept the faith, they would have made a lot more money.

One way to keep control of your distributors is

to make sure they never get their hands on the
money until you say they get their hands on
the money. If you have to send something back
or the distributor didn't actually sell the five hundred dozen he thought he would, you will be left
holding the bag if you have already paid. You
should get paid directly by the store, and then
you pay the distributors. If the distributor gets
paid, takes his commission, and hands the rest
over to you, you've got no leverage. If you haven't
paid him and you still own the goods, you're the
king. There's no limit to what he'll do for you. If
it's broken, they fix it. If it's not delivered, they
will deliver it. If a buyer claims he ordered only
five hundred dozen and the distributor delivered
a thousand, the distributor eats the difference.
Best of all, if you owe him money, he isn't going
to want you to drop your price.

You also have to be ready to cut your ties with
the distributors who aren't capable of running
with your fad in its later stages. As sad as it is, it
is a fact that the sales rep who could help you at
the mom-and-pop level just isn't going to cut it
with the national chain people. The result of this
reality is not as heartless as it sounds, because by
the time you have to move up to the next level of
distributor, the guy who started out with you has
made a nice piece of change.

You have to do this or you won't grow. Fads
are ephemeral, kind of mystical. It's there and it
isn't there and you can't put too much ballast on
it. Keep people on the payroll who you can't use
anymore, and your fad will die of its own weight.
You are not IBM, nor would you want to be. You
can't keep the guy in sales until he gets the gold
watch because he made you what you are today.
You have to keep telling yourself he wouldn't be

where he is today without you. And then you have to send him on his way. You don't have forever with a fad. To add on people, you have to drop people. It is a simple fact of fad life.

When the Wallwalker hit the *CBS Evening News*, I had to drop my local distributors right away. I could no longer supply the boutiques and newsstands in Washington. To get the national distribution I needed and to be able to promise K mart I could get them several hundred thousand in two weeks, I cut off everyone I had worked with to that point. What made it easier was that they had made a good profit on Wallwalkers, and they understood that getting the toy to the chains was a different proposition.

# Fifteen

# Knocking Off the Knockoffs: Customs Is a Fad's Best Friend

> *Arnold Schwarzenegger as the Terminator couldn't keep out the knockoffs.*

Remember the "Baby on Board" signs that swept the yuppified nation a few years ago. It's hard to figure out what it was about that statement that caught on.

The part of that story no one knows is that most of the money on that fad was not made by the poor guy who came up with the first "Baby on Board" sticker. On the contrary, that guy made very little. It was the knockoffs of the original— those signs that said "Mother-in-Law on Board," "Mother-in-Law in Trunk," and "Ex-Husband on Roof Rack" that cleaned up.

So the inventor from Chestnut Hill, Massachusetts, lost out on the part of that fad that made most of the money.

How can you keep this from happening to you? The short answer is, it is very hard. There are legal steps you can take, but you stick your finger in one hole in the dike and the water starts pouring through another. Every time that "baby on board" guy saw a car rolling down the street with a whatever-on-board sign, he must have felt sick. If he had gone after one imitator and stopped the "mother-in-law" signs, he would have had to go after another to stop the "ex-wife" signs, and on and on.

You can stop someone from taking your name with a trademark (legal rights to a name), copyright (legal rights to a design), or patent (legal rights to an invention or a process). See Chapter 10.

But you have to remember that when you talk about legal protection, you are talking about lawyers. And when you talk about lawyers you are talking money, perhaps more money than your idea will ever make. This is the dilemma: If your idea isn't hot, it isn't going to need protection. If it is hot, no matter how much legal talent you buy, you still are going to be copied. Someone who wants to imitate your product because it is hot is going to factor in the cost of being sued as the price he pays for a piece of the action.

Some of the large toy companies know that no matter how much they pay lawyers, the whole area of copying hot products is too volatile to prevent. Game companies—in particular, board game companies—won't even accept mail that looks as if it may contain a game idea. Take last year's obsession—insider trading. I can imagine how many unsolicited versions of Wall Street games Parker Brothers received, given that I got a crate of them myself. The game companies are wise to send these back unopened. They are undoubtedly working on something similar themselves, and they don't want to risk being sued by some guy who may have a lawyer somewhere busily seeking a copyright on his idea. NBC wades through more than 250,000 suggestions a year but may be reconsidering opening unsolicited mail. Last year it was sued by a man who claimed that he had sent the network the idea for *The Cosby Show*. The network won, but going into court is always an expensive nuisance.

Stop for a moment and consider what a patent

means. It takes hours of a lawyer's time, and then what do you have? Here are the statistics: Only five of every hundred patents issued end up as products. Of those five, only a fraction become part of a product that ends up on a shelf somewhere. And a smaller fraction yet of that small fraction become part of a product that ends up on a shelf somewhere and actually makes money. The only person getting rich off most patents is the lawyer filing for them.

Even when you have legal protection and even when you go into court to enforce it and even when you win, you don't always win. Take Gary Dahl, who obtained all the appropriate copyrights and a trademark for the Pet Rock. When Dahl found out that a Canadian company was knocking off the Pet Rock, he promptly sued. He won a judgment. Winning that judgment cost him $25,000 in legal fees, not counting the money he spent getting the copyright and trademark in the first place. But he never saw a dime because the company he sued went bankrupt. Knockoff companies are notoriously undercapitalized and transient. You can win, but often you can't collect.

This is not to say that other people capitalizing on your idea isn't a terrible problem. There were copies of the Wallwalker starting ten days after the *CBS Evening News* piece ran. I called K mart to see if they had received my package to them after sending samples by Federal Express. The buyer told me he already had twelve different samples of Wallwalkers on his desk from various people. I said, "How can that be?" It turns out that some of these people didn't even have the decency to send prototypes of their own. They just sent my Wallwalker as their own. Open for business and ready to accept orders.

These copycats knew that by the time they got a K mart order, they could be geared up to manufacture their own version.

The problem is so bad that a former buyer for one of the chain stores told me that the vice-president for merchandise of that chain sent one of my Wallwalkers to Taiwan and ordered two million direct from the factory. He was willing to risk being sued in order to get a better price from one of the knockoff factories.

Since lawyers can't eliminate this behavior and you won't have much money to fool around with, hold off on the lawyers until you know you have a hot product. Now, lawyers will get upset about this because you should have protection from the outset and because it cuts into the money they can make. When you know something is hot, spend the $5,000 and get all the protection you can. (See Chapter 10, "Let's Get Legal.")

Your legal problems are made easier if you are dealing with a domestic product. You can pinpoint where the object is being made—say, Omaha—and shut them down. What is hard is when the product comes from abroad, which most do these days.

Take fake Rolexes, one of the favorites of the knockoff artists in the Far East. You just aren't going to be able to police a factory in Taiwan as easily as you can one in Nebraska. The laws are different. And it's much harder to monitor what's going on halfway around the world. You can't afford to have investigators dropping in.

You are up against five factories in Taiwan, two in Hong Kong, and four in Korea, all making knockoffs faster than you can. All are being exported by three hundred small trading companies in those countries to three hundred importers in the United States. They, in turn, are distributing to twenty thousand stores across the country. This is much harder to police than one single factory in Omaha.

Even if you can shut down three factories in Taiwan, three new factories will spring up down the street tomorrow morning. You have to keep fighting, but the longer your fad lasts, the more of a losing battle it becomes.

In my case, as soon as I obtained the legal U.S. rights, I went to U.S. Customs. I filed with all the ports of entry, and there are many of them. To those who say the bureaucracy doesn't work, I point to Mrs. Lane with customs in Washington. She is the savior of a lot of small business in this country. She took the time to wire Hawaii, San Francisco, Los Angeles, Seattle, Chicago, and New York to let them know the Wallwalker was mine and not to let any others in. If she hadn't done that, many more knockoffs would have slipped in.

Then I had my lawyer send a copy by Federal Express to eighty smaller ports of entry, notifying them of the same thing.

It wasn't until recently that a fad product could get much real help from customs. For that we can thank E.T. That poor character had been knocked off from coast to coast before the closing credits of the Universal movie. U.S. Customs hadn't dealt with a problem like this before and didn't know what to do. After that fiasco, customs beefed up a special section to deal with hot items—in other words, fads. Now you can say I have a hot item and get fast action. You have to get them to agree with you that it's hot, but that's not too hard. The presumption is that you aren't going to go to the bother of slogging through the U.S. bureaucracy if you don't have something hot to protect. Anyway, customs agents don't live in monasteries.

Sometimes a company like J. C. Penney will order an item before you have had a chance to file legal rights to it. They will check beforehand with U.S. Customs to see if they can bring in an item, and customs, unaware of a pending application, will say yes. There is nothing on the books. Something may have been filed at the patent office but not made it to U.S. Customs. Or it made it to U.S. Customs but not the right office in the hinterlands. If J. C. Penney's order was made *before* your application was on the books but arrives *after* your application has been approved, they will be very upset to be told that it can't come in because it interferes with someone's legal rights.

One day after I had filed all the appropriate papers with customs, my wife got a call about a block order coming into San Francisco. The caller said he had been stopped from bringing the Wallwalkers in by U.S. Customs, which told the importer to call the holder of the legal rights.

My wife put him on hold. We jumped up and down celebrating while his shipment was stuck in the dock at San Francisco. The seal I had hoped we placed around the perimeter of the country was working. This was a great day.

Well, it turned out not to be as great a day as we thought. There would be many more calls and there would be calls that didn't come, meaning many Wallwalkers were slipping through. Customs occasionally seizes a shipment and burns it as a deterrent to others (customs sends the rights owner a bill for the incineration) without giving the importer a chance to talk to the rights owner.

There are a number of ways to handle the calls

that come from importers caught at the docks. You can simply refuse to let the shipment in. Or you can negotiate with the importer. You have him in a great position. You have all the bargaining strength, since he faces two choices: losing his shipment entirely, because you tell customs to send it back to Taiwan or wherever, or because customs sets a match to the whole crate right then and there; or he can pay you to let it in. In my case, this meant signing over a large part of the profit to me. The importer is willing to do that because at least that way he gets back his cost.

There were a few who didn't want to pay, and they had to return the shipment to Taiwan. Most decided to salvage their costs and turn the shipment over to me. There were so many of these situations that my lawyer and I had a small cottage industry in port-of-entry licensing. We turned out to be licensing the knockoffs.

But this is better than their just coming in willy-nilly. You get something—indeed, a lot—of the profit from it. You deter others from doing it when word gets around. And you save the price on your product. If many of these knockoffs get in, you will see the price on your product go into free fall. K mart and their ilk will be furious!

Unfortunately, the protection you try to give the retailer isn't always a two-way street. If the buyer at a chain has the chance to buy your product at a lower price, he's going to grab it. He could care less whether it's the original or not as long as he doesn't get caught. A buyer isn't going to get fired for violating your legal protection, but he is going to get fired for paying a higher price than his competitor at the next mall.

Knockoffs always are going to be part of the fad world. No matter how many lawyers you hire and no matter how airtight your rights, knockoffs are going to get in. As one customs official said, "Ken, we can't keep out the heroin. We can't keep out the cocaine. How do you expect us to keep out a bunch of toys?"

# Sixteen

# Keeping the Engine Running:
# How to Turn a Fad into a Classic

> Greta Garbo knew something that the Cabbage Patch Kids didn't: Overexposure will make you red hot, but you burn out. Underexposure will make you a legend.

Fads are born to die. As I said before, in Fad Standard Time, a day is a month, and a fad that lasts two months is a classic.

But you want your fad to be one of the exceptions to FST, to become a classic like the Slinky or the Frisbee. You will have to ignore the current fashion in the marketplace to slash and burn: to saturate the market, bombard the public, milk it to the last drop, and get out.

Ignore it, because with vigilance and a willingness to leave the stage before they give you the hook, you can be one of the ones that last. Look at the fads that have turned into classics by not following the get-rich-quick approach. The Slinky, which has been thriving for forty-three years, began as a fad. The yo-yo, the Frisbee, and Silly Putty have all been around for several decades. No one milked these products.

Take the Frisbee. It has survived long after the original craze that set off its sales boom in 1957. Hardly a man, woman, or child alive today doesn't know what to do with a Frisbee. The joy of whirling a plastic disk through the air to be snared by another pair of hands has never lost its appeal. We know that Knerr and Melin distributed thousands of these products to kids, recreation departments, boys' clubs, the Girl Scouts, and the like. But those wily inventors went even farther to assure that their toy would become an enduring part of the sports scene. They formed the International Frisbee Association to organize competitions. The best was called Ultimate Frisbee, a kind of relay race using the flying disk where two teams move down the field to a goalpost while throwing disks back and forth across the field. World Frisbee Disk Championships included every kind of sport devised for a ball, only using a Frisbee: tennis, golf, dance, distance throwing. The latest is dog-catch competitions, in which a person throws a Frisbee to a dog, who catches it in his mouth, or in which he throws it to another person, who catches it with his mouth. Fanatics organize their own events modeled after the sanctioned events. Each year the Washington Monument grounds is the scene of what its organizers call the Olympics of Frisbee. Altogether, well over a hundred million have been sold, and sales of several hundred thousand a year continue.

In general, there is not enough belief in products these days to engender much loyalty. Mattel, American Greetings, and Coleco realize their products have very little intrinsic appeal. To them a new product is about as seductive as a new laundry detergent. They know the public is going to tire of a product, because they have already tired of it themselves.

This is the lot of products created with the lowest common denominator in mind, the product designed to offend the fewest number of people. Corporate America feels safer producing this rather than something that will strongly appeal to 30 percent of the population—say, Batman and

Robin—and offend the rest of the populace. You can guess that about half the people in the United States are going to hate Batman, Robin, Batmobiles, and all the rest of it.

That's what happens with strong characters. An American toy company doesn't want to develop a strong character that could create negative feelings, even if the flip side is very positive feelings in a small segment.

Group think ruins most products. There is no guiding force falling in love, as I did with the Wallwalker. Instead, some guy in marketing comes up with a slapped-together character, another guy in a green eyeshade crunches some numbers, and the vice-president for new projects says to go with it.

Great fads start with a light bulb going off in someone's head. No market research at all. Any cuteness that attaches is intrinsic, not bolted on.

With Wallwalkers, I am not like some creative director at American Greetings. I want to see it become a classic American toy. I want it to be my contribution to American pop culture. Maybe there will be a Wallwalker at the Smithsonian someday, right beside Mr. Greenjeans' pipe and the O.R. from *MASH*.

You don't want your creation to crash and die. It's a living creature to you, after all. Land it clean and your fad can come back. Keep it at a cruising altitude and it may never land at all.

With the Wallwalker, when sales were tapering off after about eighteen months, everyone advised me to go for it, sell everything I could in the next few months, discount as much as necessary, use up inventory, and get out.

This was an attractive idea because NBC had just aired a prime-time cartoon special starring a bunch of Wallwalkers during Christmastime in 1983. Right after that, people were knocking down my door to license Wallwalkers: Wacky Wallwalker lunch boxes, Wacky Wallwalker dolls, Wacky Wallwalker sheets. If I had exploited all those opportunities, I probably would have made another $1 million in up-front royalties. If I had asked a big consultant what I should do, he would have said to go for it.

But I knew that if I licensed it, I would kill it. I couldn't bear the thought of thousands of Wallwalker lunch boxes and flashlights in a huge Dollar Bin at K mart. I have seen piles of E.T. products on the bargain shelf, and it's kind of sad.

So I decided not to accept any of the licensing offers. What's more, I decided to pull all Wallwalkers off the market. It was the only way I knew to keep Wallwalkers from self-destructing in an orgy of sales. I have never been sorry, became Wallwalkers did get a new lease on life. In fact, three years after their debut, it was still enough of a phenomenon to land an appearance on the *Today* show in 1985, being compared to the Slinky.

I wanted to make the Wallwalker hard to get, make it scarce, make it something people had to seek out. I did this by cutting off all retail sales. By 1985 there was hardly a Wallwalker to be seen on the shelf on any chain store in the country. The item had cooled off enough that the knockoffs had left. I then looked at the large corporations that offer toys as premiums. Companies like Kellogg or McDonald's or Wendy's are looking for a toy with a lot of name recognition and perceived value so that a parent will be willing to pay $2 for a box of cereal. I could tell Kellogg not only that the Wallwalker was worth

$2.00 but also that the only way to get one was out of a cereal box.

In fact, I created new demand by making Wallwalkers scarce. People wrote and called asking where they could get Wallwalkers, which they had become hooked on.

The strategy worked because the Wallwalker premium was one of the most successful in Kellogg history.

Earlier Wendy's offered Wallwalkers as a premium for 99 cents with the purchase of a bag of french fries. With both companies I not only got the sales from the Wallwalker going in with the product but also about $10 million worth of national advertising I never could have purchased.

There is a lesson here. People get oversaturated. Who wants to see Michael Jackson's face on a TV commercial every day? You have to play the underexposure game. If someone walks into a store and sees a Wallwalker after not being able to find one for several months, or sees it on the back of Kellogg's Corn Flakes, he or she is going to get excited and buy it.

This is a hard strategy to pursue. You have to have a strong product to begin with and a lot of faith in its intrinsic, enduring appeal. People might not see it for a year, but it rests somewhere happily in the back of their minds. The association is good. Then about a year later, they see it somewhere in a big national promotion in a cereal ad and they say, "Hey, I loved those things and I haven't seen one for a long time. I better get one."

Think of all the items that could have become classics if they hadn't been milked to death. The Smurfs, blue dwarfs who live in the forest, the creation of a Belgian artist, were successful as a

Saturday morning cartoon show, but the Smurf doll is dead. The creators licensed everything from Smurf sweat shirts to Smurf mugs and made some quick money, but they blew the chance to create a doll with the endurance of a Disney character. They got greedy, overexposed the character, and ended up with a Strawberry Shortcake situation.

Another example is the Cabbage Patch Kids. They had a shot at becoming the new Raggedy Ann, Paddington Bear, or Barbie. But because of the mass marketing and the media hype, which perhaps they couldn't control, it got out of hand. It burned out after two years. They blew the chance to become a classic doll. Instead they have a mass doll that no one wants anymore.

A good fad toy is like Frank Sinatra. It retires for a while, then makes another comeback. Richard Knerr has found that every seven or eight years the fad cycle can be renewed because there's a whole new crop of kids.

Also, playthings benefit from what NBC Entertainment president Brandon Tartikoff calls the evergreen market, his term for the children's market. As a child grows older, he sees the same toy again and again, at each stage through different eyes. You want a Frisbee at age five for different reasons than at age twelve and then for different reasons again when you are in college. Then you turn around and buy one for your children. Even adults have nostalgia kicks over some treasured toys. Those Slinkys and Frisbees in the office aren't there accidentally.

There is such a thing as fad immortality. I'm going for it. My greatest hope is that one of your grandchildren will pop into the house someday and throw one of my Wallwalkers on your wall.

# Seventeen

# Getting Paid

Hold the champagne until the check clears.

Say you're doing really well. You've racked up a lot of orders—$50,000 in one trade show, and orders are coming in at a good pace.

I would wait a while before I went out to celebrate. How long would I wait? Well, at least sixty days. That's how long it takes to get paid and have the checks cleared.

That old saw "Your check is in the mail" is going to drive you to distraction. The lag time in paying that helped you in the beginning when you needed to place orders and contract for transportation on credit hurts when you are on the receiving end. It's easier for Flying Tiger air freight to carry you than for you to carry a gift shop in San Francisco.

Small storefront retail operations are notorious for going out of business—just disappearing overnight. Owners may mean well, but when they see their whole business going to ruin, your problems recede in importance. On top of that a proprietor in San Francisco knows that you aren't going to race out from your place of business in Kansas City and demand the $284 for the three dozen Lucite cookbook holders he owes you. He can afford to be casual in his payments.

Other ways you end up not being paid is on remainders. If a product does not move off the shelf right away, some retailers will remove it and leave you holding the bag. They will ship you the remainders—C.O.D. And remainders are exactly what they sound like, leftovers that have been sitting on the shelf getting dirty, broken if they can break. Often they have price stickers that can't be removed short of a blowtorch. These are not products that can be turned around and shipped to another customer. This is the reality of small accounts.

Larger stores will have different reasons for not paying you on time, but the result is the same: You're left hanging. One of the problems with the larger stores is that they negotiate excellent discounts for themselves—they have a lot of leverage, after all—and then take the discount without carrying out their end of the deal. For example, let's say you were willing to grant a 2 percent discount in exchange for payment within ten days, a standard agreement known as a 2-10 in the trade. Thirty days pass by. You call. By this time the whole payment is due and you say, "Where is my money?" They say, "Hold on, the authorization has already gone to accounting. Don't be such a pain in the neck." What do you think the chances are that you are going to get payment in full? That you are going to get payment in full the day or the week after that phone call?

Chances are good that you will get payment less a 2 percent discount in sixty days and you will say "Thank you very much." That's because you can't afford to tick these guys off. At the beginning of the Wallwalkers, I was able to get letters of credit from the major chains guaranteeing payment. That's in part what allowed me to move ahead without sufficient capital. But at that time they needed me more than I needed them. When it switches back, they will pay you, but in their own sweet time.

There are ways to prevent some of the payment problems that are endemic in the retail industry. If you are selling to mom-and-pop stores, screen them first. Use a company like Dun & Bradstreet to do a credit rating for you. You can skip the credit rating step if you are using one of the large distribution companies (see Appendix 3) that keeps its own in-house record of payment. They will not ship to customers who are behind in their bills. Often this is more efficient in that the records are more accurate and up-to-date than those of credit rating bureaus.

Another way is to sell to your accounts C.O.D. In exchange for customers accepting shipment this way, grant a 5 percent discount. You will come out ahead. If you are worried that the checks may not be good, insist on cashier's checks. Then you are protected.

One of the best ways to ensure payment is to contract the whole system out without any strings attached. Use UPS. The company not only runs a wonderful delivery system, it also runs a wonderful collection system. With one phone call to a customer representative, you can set up an account. This entitles you to use the service to ship your goods. UPS collects upon delivery. It doesn't cost you any more to have them deliver this way. Make sure your account is set up so that only cashier's checks will be accepted.

Collection agencies take such a huge percentage of whatever they can collect that I stay away from them. It's more effective to keep it personal.

I also have found that most people want to pay in the end. With small operations, you'll find that after a few phone calls your check will be in the mail.

# Eighteen

# Getting Discovered

Fad Fair can make you a star, and not just for fifteen minutes.

Let's face it: You can't have a fad without being discovered. That's why I created Fad Fair. It gives everybody in the country the same opportunity for fame and fortune. It's kind of like an audition—a fadster's chorus line. Not everyone is going to make it big, but you greatly improve your chances.

Fad Fair—the showcase of faddom—lets the whole world in on your idea all at once. It started in Detroit in January 1986, in the ballroom of the Westin Hotel, with twenty-seven fad exhibitors. We were hoping for a couple hundred visitors. We got fifteen hundred in one afternoon and had to turn people away. When I was organizing the fair, I had thought we would have enough room to accommodate the crowd, but I really underestimated Fad Fair's appeal.

The following year in January we expanded our quarters to Detroit's Cobo Hall Convention Center. Seventy-five hopeful fadsters rented space to display their wares. And sixteen thousand people—thirty per minute clocked at the door— came to see what was going on. We had figured if we got four thousand we'd be doing great.

And all this without spending one dime on

advertising—all the attention came through the media. I've said it before but I can't stress it enough: The best kind of exposure is free—not only because you don't have to spend time planning it and money paying for it, but also because the public, saturated by commercials and skeptical of them, gives far more weight to a news story.

The local and national radio and TV shows covered Fad Fair like a blanket—before, during, and after. Even the jaded members of the press will get behind a fad. It makes their jobs easier, of course, to have something noncontroversial to fill their news hole, but they also like to root for the little guy with nothing but a shoeshine and smile. It's the American Dream; it's Rocky. It's the notion that "Hey! If it happened to him, it could happen to me."

Readers identify with the people at Fad Fair. Unlike winning the Nobel Prize in Medicine, any couch potato in the country can start a fad. I did twenty-eight interviews and lost count of the number of interviews individual fadsters took part in.

As the site of the first Fad Fair, Detroit was a natural. Most of my Fad Hotline calls in the early days came from the area around Michigan and Illinois. Detroit seemed to be the Silicon Valley of Fads.

But by November 1987 it was time to move on. More and more people were calling to reserve a booth at Fad Fair, and many were from the East Coast. And although we were getting great coverage in Detroit, the big break for fads always is a national one. The opportunity for national coverage is vastly greater in New York.

There was a huge risk in taking the show to Broadway. A lot of public-relations people said we would bomb, that what flew in Detroit probably wouldn't make it in the Big Apple.

But I took the risk and rented the second-largest convention space in the city at New York's Sheraton Centre on Broadway for November 13 and 14, 1987. Even though reservations were pouring in for space all through the fall, I was apprehensive that the move to New York might ruin the magical chemistry of Fad Fair.

Not true. Going into Fad Fair '87, we had over 100 exhibitors, over five times the number at the first Fad Fair. I had the feeling that something big could happen in New York. There was an electricity in the air that had been missing in Detroit.

It turned out that the move to New York gave Fad Fair the national exposure it needed to enter the big time. Where else but in New York can you be seen by all the major toy companies at once, all the chain store buyers, all those media people looking for FUN things to write about? Until New York, Fad Fair averaged about thirty reporters. We sent press credentials for admission to Sheraton Centre for over a hundred reporters from newspapers, radio, and television. Fad Fair got feature coverage in everything from *Money* magazine to *Vogue* to *The Village Voice*. We even got a five-minute feature on National Public Radio. The front page of the second section of *The New York Times*, NBC's *Today* show and the *CBS Morning News* ran features. Producers from the David Letterman show were checking out a number of fadsters.

One key to the attraction of Fad Fair to the media is critical mass. One fad person doesn't necessarily have enough to offer *The New York Times* or *USA Today*. But if one hundred fad hopefuls are gathered in one place, the reporters see one hundred potential human-interest features there for the taking. No phone calls, no scheduling interviews, no running all over the city chasing people down. Reporters are as lazy as the next person, and the easier you make it for them, the more likely you are to get a story out of them.

Even though New York makes Fad Fair a natural for national coverage, it still is a bonanza for the local media, who are anxious for "hometown boy makes good in the big city" stories.

I also supply a news hook for reporters who need one by awarding each year a Faddy for lifetime achievement. Past winners have been Betty James; Richard Knerr and Spud Melin; and Ruth and Elliot Handler, the parents of Barbie and Ken.

Fad Fair costs about $100,000 to put on, and I take in about $50,000 from the fadsters who come and rent space—many who can't afford the going rate get a discount—which means I lose about $50,000 on the deal. This is my contribution to fad people. It wouldn't be hard to break even on Fad Fair. All it would take is to jack up the price of a booth to $1,000. I would still get a good turnout, but the fun would be gone. The very people I want to attract wouldn't be able to afford it, and the whole thing would turn into something else—something mainstream. One thing the world doesn't need is another trade show where established companies get to show their wares, for a price, usually about $1,500 at a place comparable to New York's Sheraton Centre.

I checked out a few of these trade shows in New York: the Gift Show, Toy Fair, the Stationery Show—and at first I thought, my God, all these interesting novelty items looking suspiciously like—well, fads. But on closer look I realized that these things aren't fads and that this isn't what Fad Fair is all about. It's kind of like Hallmark trying to make "alternative" greeting cards in the Sandra Boynton mode. It just doesn't come off. The people with booths at the Gift Show are a breed apart from the people who take a booth at Fad Fair. It's the kid with the lemonade stand vs. General Foods.

I think of Fad Fair as a challenge to Toy Fair, which should be a creative exchange of ideas but which has grown into a huge, unimaginative, corporate event tailored to the big companies. Toy Fair took the fun out of toys; Fad Fair puts it back in.

The whole point of Fad Fair is to give the individual a chance—the typist from Staten Island, the truck driver from Dallas, the factory worker from Ohio, the stockbroker from L.A. That's why I started Fad Scholarships. If someone can't raise enough money to exhibit at Fad Fair, I let them come for a quarter of the going rate. And kids with a fad to exhibit get a booth free. Fad Fair in New York is going to be an annual event each November or December.

# Nineteen

# Call for Help: The Fad Hotline

> The Fad Hotline is my version of Dialing for Dollars. When people realize they are calling Washington, D.C., they think they have reached the U.S. Department of Fads.

Legitimate advice is hard to find. I discovered this when I started out. Fad marketing is unique, and mainstream marketing rules don't apply. As I discussed in Chapter 7: "Getting Your Act Together," it's best to avoid the advicemongers who offer for a fee to get your business started. When I started out, I had no one to turn to. It never occurred to me to call up Betty James of Slinky fame or Richard Knerr from Wham-O, so I was surprised when would-be fadsters started calling me soon after my success with the Wallwalker.

Before I knew it, the phone was ringing constantly. With all the publicity I was getting with Wallwalkers, I was becoming a lightning rod for people who had interesting ideas and were looking for information. There wasn't a course at Harvard Business School devoted to fad marketing, but it was looking as if there was enough interest in the field to justify it.

I decided it would be interesting to serve as an Ann Landers for fadsters, so I went to the phone company and got an 800 number for a hotline. I know a long-distance phone charge can sometimes be enough to stymie a budding fadster, and

I wanted to make it easy to call, something that would be fun to do.

Fortunately, the phone company was able to give me an 800 number with USA in it. Most of the variations on that theme as you might expect had already been taken. But USA-FADS was still available.

I started giving the number out during talk show interviews, and before long I was getting thirty calls a day. Then, during the months before the first Fad Fair, which was getting a lot of publicity, I was getting as many as eight hundred calls a day.

The Fad Hotline averages about two hundred calls a day now, more than I can keep up with. One reason I'm writing this book is to answer some of those calls.

# Twenty

# Dr. Fad's Guide to Life: Random Tips from the Father of the Wacky Wallwalker

> The fad mentality is a way of life. You have to see the world differently than other people see it, step to the beat of your own drummer. You have to live, eat, and breathe your fad.

### 1. A Fad is not a Vegematic.

If it slices and dices and broils and boils, it's not a fad. A fad only slices.

### 2. But wait—there's less.

One of the things I hear most when I'm talking to would-be fadmakers is that old lament, "As soon as I've gotten my gizmo just a little better (a little cuter, a little shinier, a little uglier, a little bouncier—you fill in the blank), then I'll be ready."

When it comes to fads, less is more. Often, tinkering is a symptom of birth pangs, a fear of letting your baby out of the garage. The improvement you are looking for might just complicate matters; at the very least it wastes valuable time. Stick with that shade of purple. You're not selling aesthetics. Whether something bounces 20 percent higher or goes 20 percent faster or looks 20 percent better is not what you are after. You are going after the "big WOW factor."

### 3. Keep it short.

The media have a shorter attention span than I do. For radio and TV you need a fifteen-second explanation. Nothing looks sillier than some poor slob on a talk show trying to demonstrate a new product and the director drawing his finger across his throat and the host saying, "Well, our time is up" and you're in the middle of your spiel. Meanwhile, the host could care less; all he's thinking about is a clever segue into a commercial, and the whole point is lost. If you get more than fifteen seconds, you can always show it off again.

### 4. Avoid high-tech, high-gloss.
Fads are definitely low-tech operations. High-gloss is for Madison Avenue, where they can afford it. Your only chance is to go 180 degrees in the opposite direction to total low-gloss. Break out the Magic Markers and handwrite your own brochure—the hokier the better.

### 5. Every sample is worth a thousand words.
Everyone loves a freebie, especially if it's fun. Samples don't cost you much and they say more than ten press releases.

### 6. Never send out anything that says, "Some assembly required."
I get samples all the time that have to be put together. I say to myself, "Some other time, maybe if I live to be a hundred, I'll get to this thing" and file it away in the bottom drawer. Sending a sample that requires anything of the person receiving it is not much better than sending nothing at all. Do you think the buyer at the Sharper Image or Neiman-Marcus is going to take the time to figure out how to assemble and display your product? Not on your life. One fadster was trying to launch an inflatable globe by sending it to potential buyers in a tiny envelope. I told him the buyer at Bloomingdale's wasn't going to sit in his office and burst his lungs trying to blow the thing up to see what it was. I convinced him to

ship his brainchild all blown up in a huge wooden crate. Suddenly he got the attention he wanted—and a wave of orders.

### 7. Ditto "batteries not included."
If it takes batteries, send them. If they need to be installed, install them (see tip 6). Don't expect anybody to do anything but open the package.

### 8. Write and rewrite directions, if any are needed, until a six-year-old could understand them.
Never include more than two lines of directions. One line is better. "Throw this at the wall" or "Put this on your head" will do nicely.

### 9. Never use jargon in press interviews.
If you use terms like "cash flow" and "inventory," you become just like every other businessman.

### 10. Don't sweat the details.
Concentrate on the big things—there are more than enough of them. You can't be bothered with cash flows, spreadsheets, and frequent-flier miles.

### 11. Don't invest in a sequel.
Unlike Beverly Hills Cop II, there will never be Pet Sand, a Hula-Ring, or Wallrunner. Who ever heard a word about Rubik's Magic Puzzle? I rest my case.

### 12. Do exaggerate.
A fad is an exaggeration in itself. When you are talking about it, you have to use extreme terms.

### 13. Don't name-drop.
You don't want to be establishment or a celebrity. You are one lone guy out there with a shoeshine and a smile and no connections. You are just like the person buying your fad and hoping to launch one of his own someday. Claiming to know Cher's road manager is out of character and tacky.

### 14. Don't be linear.

A fad is a merry-go-round. One minute it's a catalog item, another it's at K mart, then it's a cartoon special, then it's a premium at Wendy's. Any one of them can happen anytime if you keep your mind open.

### 15. Think big.

Fad people are big dreamers but small thinkers. Often they are so happy to see their widget out there that they want to send a thank-you note to anyone who buys it. Believe you are going to sell millions, and people will pay more—and buy more.

### 16. Don't hold back.

You are your fad. Don't dress up like a pizza, but don't be reluctant to flail away about your fad to anyone, anytime. I threw Wallwalkers against the wall of some of the finest restaurants in the country.

### 17. Don't take the pros' advice as gospel.

They've had some successes, true. But their mistakes are hidden. You don't hear about the chance they didn't take. They are cautious and will preach caution to you.

### 18. Keep it fun.

A fad is fun. Remember that. It isn't useful, it isn't going to cure cancer. The veep at Kenner Toys can afford to be a grim green eyeshade type because he isn't his fad. If the fun goes out of your fad, it dies.

### 19. Act like an amateur, sting like a pro.

Even if you get successful and can afford the secretary with the British accent, resist. Don't drop your amateur ways or people will think they've been had.

# Appendices

# Appendix I

## Testing Labs and Organizations

Testing labs are independent companies that will test your product for safety. Do this for your own peace of mind—you don't want your great idea to end up injuring someone. Also do it to make sure you are in compliance with the standards of the Consumer Product Safety Commission, which sets guidelines for consumer products. Should your product be involved in an accident, a certificate of compliance from a testing lab will serve as *prima facie* evidence that you made a good-faith effort to ensure your product's safety. If you have questions about how the Consumer Product Safety Commission affects your product, call the CPSC Hotline at 800-638-CPSC.

ACTS Testing
3916 Broadway Avenue
Buffalo, NY 14227
(716) 684-3300

American Association for
  Laboratory Accreditation
Gaithersburg, MD 20877
(301) 670-1377
*Has a list of accredited testing
  laboratories by state.*

Lancaster Laboratories
2425 New Holland Pike
Lancaster, PA 17601
(717) 656-2301

U.S. Testing Company
Consumer Product
  Compliance Division
1415 Park Avenue
Hoboken, NJ 07030
(201) 792-2400

# Appendix 2

## Patent and Inventor Organizations

Listed below are organizations that can help you in securing patents, trademarks, and copyrights. For general information, of course, the best place to call is the U.S. Office of Patents and Trademarks, (703) 557-3158. Also listed are private organizations that seek to help budding inventors with their projects.

### Patent, Trademark, and Copyright Organizations

American Copyright Council
Washington, DC
(202) 293-1966

American Copyright Society
New York, NY
(212) 582-5705

American Intellectual
Property Law Association
Arlington, VA
(703) 521-1680

International Licensing
Industry and
Merchandisers' Association
New York, NY
(212) 244-1944

International Patent and
Trademark Association
Chicago, IL
(312) 641-1500

Inventors Workshop
International Education
Foundation
Tarzana, CA
(818) 344-3375
*Provides instruction, assistance, and guidance in such areas as patent protection; how to get inventions designed, production engineered, and manufactured; and how to offer inventions for sale.*

National Council of Patent
  Law Associations
Office of Public Affairs—U.S.
  Patent and Trade Office
Arlington, VA
(703) 557-3341

National Patent Council
Arlington, VA
(703) 521-1669

Patent and Trademark Office
  Society
Arlington, VA
(703) 557-2173

Society of University Patent
  Administrators
Ames, IA
(515) 294-4740

United States Office of
  Patents and Trademarks
Arlington, VA
(703) 557-3158

United States Trademark
  Association
New York, NY
(212) 986-5880

## Inventors' Organizations

American Association of
  Inventors
Bridgeport, MI
(517) 799-8208

American Society of Inventors
Philadelphia, PA
(215) 546-6601

Inventors Association of
  America
Rancho Cucamonga, CA
(714) 980-6446
*Assists members in patenting,
  producing, and marketing
  their ideas. Maintains a
  Board of Evaluators to
  judge the quality and
  potential of members'
  creations; aims to thwart
  efforts by large corporations
  to improve or manufacture
  members' inventions and
  thereby obtain patents.*

Invention Marketing Institute
Glendale, CA
(818) 246-6540
*Association to help inventors
  get their products into
  the marketplace and to
  help manufacturers find
  new products to make and
  market.*

Inventors' Clubs of America
Altanta, GA
(404) 938-5089
*Stimulates inventiveness and
  helps inventors in all
  phases of their work,
  including patenting,
  development, manufac-
  turing, marketing, and
  advertising. Seeks to
  prevent abuses to the
  individual inventor, such
  as theft of ideas.*

National Congress of
    Inventors' Organizations
Rheem Valley, CA
(415) 376-7541

National Inventors'
    Foundation
Glendale, CA
(818) 246-6540
*Educates individuals with
    regard to the protection
    and promotion of inventions
    and new products.*

Society for the Encouragement
    of Research and Invention
Summit, NJ
(201) 273-1088

U.S. Patent Model
    Foundation
Washington, DC
(202) 737-1836
*Seeks to enhance public
    awareness of American
    inventions, both past and
    present.*

# Appendix 3

## Major Chain Stores, Major Distributors, and Toy Buyers

You can get a good start on getting your product into the appropriate retail channels with this list of the country's major chain stores, the major distributors to those stores, and top buyers of toys, and the kind and number of outlets. This is not a complete list of all of these entities, but it is the best list.

### Major Chain Stores

#### Arkansas

Wal-Mart Stores Inc. (Disc.—768)
P.O. Box 116
702 S.W. Eighth Street
Bentonville, 72712
(501) 273-4000

#### California

Alpha Beta Markets (Sup.—339)
777 S. Harbor Boulevard
La Habra, 90631
(714) 738-2000

Circle K (Sup.—3,144)
(Western Region)
2588 Newport Boulevard
Costa Mesa, 92627
(714) 752-8118

Hub Distributing (Var.—305)
(Miller's Outpost)
2501 Guasti Road
Ontario, 91761
(714) 988-6431

K mart Apparel Corp. (Disc.—1,885)
23000 S. Avalon Boulevard
Carson, 90745
(213) 549-4700

McCrory Stores (Var. and
  Dep't.—800)
11211 Van Owen Street
North Hollywood, 91605
(213) 877-0432


Safeway Stores Inc.
  (Sup.—2,100)
2800 Ygnacio Valley Road
Walnut Creek, 94598
(415) 944-4100


Sprouse-Reitz Co. (Var.—330)
1313 W. 8th Street
Los Angeles, 90017
(213) 413-8161


Thrifty Drug and Discount
  Stores (Drug—561)
3425 Wilshire Boulevard
Los Angeles, 90010
(213) 251-6000


Value Fair (Disc., Drug, and
  Sup.—339)
444. E. Lambert Road
Fullerton, 92635
(714) 738-2741


Woolco (Disc.—305)
112 W. Ninth Street
Los Angeles, 90015
(212) 625-8647


## Connecticut

Ames Department Stores
  (Disc. and Var.—468)
2418 Main Street
Rocky Hill, 06067
(203) 563-8234

## Florida

Certified Grocers of Florida
  (Coop.—1,700)
P.O. Box 1510
8305 S.E. 58th Avenue
Ocala, 32678
(904) 245-5151


Eckerd Drug Corp. (Drug—
  1,740)
P.O. Box 4689
(8333 Bryan Dairy Road)
Clearwater, 33518
(813) 397-7461


Shop and Go (Sup.—410)
P.O. Box 428
Mango, 33550
(813) 689-8161


Winn-Dixie Stores (Sup.—
  1,200)
5050 Edgewood Court
Jacksonville, 32205
(904) 783-5000


Zippy Mart (Sup.—309)
6834 Old King Road S.
Jacksonville, 32217
(904) 733-6030


## Georgia

Habersham Plantation (Gift—
  350)
P.O. Box 1209
Toccoa, 30577
(404) 886-1476

Majik Market (Sup. 1,000)
P.O. Box 7701, Station C
(1860-74 Peachtree Road
  N.W.)
Atlanta, 30357
(404) 352-6641

World Bazaar (Gift—300)
2110 Lawrence Street
East Point, 30344
(404) 766-5300

## Illinois

Ace Hardware (Hdwr.—4,600)
2200 Kensington Court
Oak Brook, 60521
(312) 990-6600

Ben Franklin Stores (Var.—
  1,700)
1700 S. Wolf Road
Des Plaines, 60018
(312) 298-8800

Cotter and Co. (Hdwr.—6,500)
(True Value Hardware)
2740 Clybourn Avenue
Chicago, 60614
(312) 975-2700

Montgomery Ward and Co.
  (Dep't.—350)
Montgomery Ward Plaza
Merchandise Building
Chicago, 60671
(312) 467-2000

Osco Drug (Drug—661)
1818 Swift Drive
Oak Brook, 60521
(312) 572-5000

Sears, Roebuck and Co.
  (Dep't.—799)
Sears Tower—Wacker Drive
Chicago, 60684
(312) 875-2500

Topco Associates Inc. (Sup.
  Coop—1,600)
7711 Grosse Pointe Road
Skokie, 60077
(312) 676-3030

V & S Variety Stores (Var.—
  over 1,100)
c/o Cotter, and Co.
2740 N. Clybourn Avenue
Chicago, 60614
(312) 975-2700

The Walgreen Co. (Drug—
  1,100)
200 Wilmot Road
Deerfield, 60015
(312) 940-2500

## Indiana

Food Marketing Corp.
  (Sup.—352)
4815 Executive Boulevard
Fort Wayne, 46808
(219) 483-2146

## Iowa

Casey's Inc. (Sup.—350)
4600 N.E. 14th Street
Des Moines, 50313
(515) 263-3700

## Kentucky

Dollar General Corp.
  (Dep't.—1,500)
P.O. Box 427
Beech Street
Scottsville, 42164
(502) 237-5444

## Maryland

Capitol Milk and High Dairy
  Stores (Sup.—340)
8920 Whiskey Bottom Road
Laurel, 20707
(301) 953-2200

## Massachusetts

Cumberland Farms Dairy
  Inc. (Sup.—1,200)
Flanders Road
Westboro, 01581
(617) 366-4445

Zayre Stores (Disc.—351)
235 Old Connecticut Path
Framingham, 01701
(617) 620-5000

## Michigan

K mart (Disc., Var.—2,484)
3100 W. Big Beaver
Troy, 48084
(313) 643-1000

Spartan Stores (Sup.—450)
P.O. Box 8700
850 76th Street S.W.
Grand Rapids, 49508
(616) 878-2000

## Minnesota

Coast to Coast Stores
  (Hdwr.—1,079)
10801 Red Circle Drive
Minnetonka, 55343
(612) 935-1711

Farwell Ozmun Kirk and Co.
  (Hdwr.—600)
411 Farwell Avenue
South St. Paul, 55075
(612) 450-5523

Northwestern Drug Co.
  (Drug—1,050)
2001 Kennedy Street N.E.
Minneapolis, 55440
(612) 331-6550

Our Own Hardware Co.
  (Hdwr.—1,000)
2300 W. Highway 13
Burnsville, 55337
(612) 890-2700

Super-Valu Stores
  (Sup.—3,360)
11840 Valley View Road
Eden Prairie, 55344
(612) 828-4000

Target Stores (Disc.—301)
P.O. Box 1392
33 S. Sixth Street
Minneapolis, 55440
(612) 370-6073

United Hardware Distributing
  Co. (Hdwr.—600)
P.O. Box 410
5005 Nathan Lane
Minneapolis, 55440
(612) 559-1800

V.S.C. Inc. (Junior Dep't.—
628)
East Highway 23, P.O.
Box E
Clara City, 56222
(612) 847-2121


## Mississippi

The Lewis Grocer Co.
(Sup.—354)
(Sunflower Stores Inc.)
Highway 49 S.
Indianola, 38751
(601) 887-3211

W.E. Walker Stores (Disc.—
329)
P.O. Box 9407
3800 I-55 N.
Jackson, 39206
(601) 981-7171


## Missouri

Hallmark Marketing (Gift—
800)
P.O. Box 419580
Kansas City, 64141
(816) 274-5111

Rexall Corp. (Drug—5,000)
3901 N. Kingshighway
St. Louis, 63115
(314) 679-7100

Western Auto (Auto—
3,400)
2107 Grand Avenue
Kansas City, 64108
(816) 346-4000


## New Jersey

A & P Food Stores (Sup.—
1,000)
2 Paragon Drive
Montvale, 07645
(201) 573-9700

Drug Guild Distributors
(Drug—400)
350 Meadowland Parkway
Secaucus, 07094
(201) 348-3700

The Grand Union (Sup.—373)
100 Broadway
Elmwood Park, 07407
(201) 794-2000

Spencer Gifts (Var—550)
1050 Black Horse Pike
Pleasantville, 08232
(609) 645-3300


## New York

Peter Schmitt Co. (Sup.—300)
355 Harlem Road
West Seneca, 14224
(716) 821-1531

F. W. Woolworth (Var.—
1,300)
233 Broadway
New York, 10279
(212) 553-2000


## North Carolina

Eckerd Drug Stores (Drug—
450)
1776 Statesville Avenue
Charlotte, 28206
(704) 371-8000

Food Lion (Sup.—327)
P.O. Box 1330
Harrison's Road
Salisbury, 28144
(704) 633-8250

The Pantry (Sup.—478)
P.O. Box 1410
1801 Douglas Drive
Sanford, 27330
(919) 776-6700

Super Dollar Stores (Disc.—327)
P.O. Box 17800
3401 Gresham's Lake Road
Raleigh, 27619
(919) 876-6000

## Ohio

American Seaway Foods
(Sup.—400)
22801 Aurora Road
Cleveland, 44146
(216) 663-5500

Gray Drug Fair (Drug—410)
668 Euclid Avenue
Cleveland 44122
(216) 566-3500

Harris General Merchandise
(Drug—300)
30600 Carter Street
Solon, 44139
(216) 248-8100

The Kroger Co. (Sup.—1,300)
1014 Vine Street
Cincinnati, 45201
(513) 762-4705

Revco Drug Stores (Drug—2,044)
1925 Enterprise Parkway
Twinsburg, 44087
(216) 425-9811

Stop-N-Go Foods (Sup.—316)
12 W. Wenger Road
Englewood, 45322
(513) 836-0941

SuperX Drug Stores
(Drug—600)
175 Tri County Parkway
Cincinnati, 45246
(513) 782-3000

Things Remembered
(Gift—500)
5340 Avion Park Drive
Highland Heights, 44143
(216) 473-2000

## Oklahoma

Otasco (Auto—544)
P.O. Box 885
11333 E. Pine Street
Tulsa, 74102
(918) 437-7171

T.G. & Y. Stores (Var.—930)
P.O. Box 25967
3815 N. Santa Fe
Oklahoma City, 73125
(405) 528-3141

## Oregon

Sprouse Reitz Co. (Var.—330)
P.O. Box 8996
1411 S.W. Morrison
Portland, 97208
(503) 224-8220

United Grocers (Coop.—400)
P.O. Box 22187
6433 S.E. Lake Road
Portland, 97222
(503) 653-6330

## Pennsylvania

Acme Markets (Sup.—300)
124 N. 15th Street
Philadelphia, 19102
(215) 568-3000

McCrory Stores (Var. and
Dep't.—326)
2955 E. Market Street
York, 17402
(717) 757-8181

G. C. Murphy Co. (Var.—
350)
531 Fifth Avenue
McKeesport, 15132
(412) 675-2000

Rite Aid Corp. (Drug—
1,269)
Trindle Road and Railroad
Avenue
Shiremanstown, 17091
(717) 761-2633

Skyline Distributors
(Sup.—336)
1905 Horse Shoe Road
Lancaster, 17601
(717) 299-5271

Thrift Drug (Drug—370)
615 Alpha Drive
Pittsburgh, 15238
(412) 781-5373

## Rhode Island

Adams Drug Co. (Drug—510)
75 Sabin Street
Pawtucket, 02860
(401) 724-9500

Consumer Value Stores
(Drug—617)
1 CVS Drive
Woonsocket, 02895
(401) 765-1500

Providence Wholesale Drug
Co. (Drug—450)
200 Niantic Avenue
Providence, 02907
(401) 942-1000

## Tennessee

Malone and Hyde Inc.
(Sup.—1,200)
P.O. Box 1898
4681 Burbank
Memphis, 38101
(901) 794-8660

## Texas

Affiliated Foods Stores (Sup.
Coop.—800)
9001 Ambassador Road
Dallas, 75247
(214) 631-3010

Pier 1 Imports Inc.
(Gift—310)
301 Commerce Suite 600
Fort Worth, 76102
(817) 878-8000

The Southland Corporation
(Sup.—7,500)
2828 N. Haskell Avenue
Dallas, 75204
(214) 828-7011

Utote M (Sup.—905)
P.O. Box 22794
5200 W. Loop Street
Houston, 77027
(713) 667-7501

## Virginia

People's Drug Stores
(Drug—542)
6315 Bren Mar Drive
Alexandria, 22312
(703) 750-6100

Richfood (Sup. Coop.—740)
P.O. Box 26967
Richmond, 23261
(804) 746-6233

## Washington

West Coast Grocery
(Sup.—500)
1525 E. "D" Street
Tacoma, 98401
(206) 593-3200

## Wisconsin

Gateway Foods (Sup.—800)
P.O. Box 1957
1637 James Street
La Crosse, 54601
(608) 785-1330

## Major Distributors

## Alabama

K.A. Fisher Co. (300)
805 First Avenue S.W.
Cullman, 35055
(205) 897-2808

## Arizona

Associated Grocers—Arizona
(900)
624 25th Avenue
Phoenix, 85036
(602) 269-0311

## Arkansas

Davis Wholesale Co. (420)
P.O. Box 5717
307 W. 2nd Avenue
Pine Bluff, 71611
(501) 534-8131

## California

Davis Sales Inc. (500)
(Liberty Distributing Co.)
P.O. Box 12748
2634 S. Cherry
Fresno, 93779
(209) 486-6560

Del Mar Sales Co. (400)
P.O. Box 23016A
9630 Chesapeake Drive
San Diego, 92123
(619) 279-1300

Emco Distributors (750)
48900 Milmont Drive
Fremont, 94538
(415) 651-1100

Handy Spot (1,500)
13402 Estrella
Gardena, 90247
(213) 515-6960

Handyspot Co. of Northern
  California (800)
1960 Williams Street
San Leandro, 94577
(415) 652-9924

Alfred M. Lewis Inc. (6,000)
3021 Franklin Avenue
Riverside, 92520
(714) 684-0170

Orange Empire (1,000)
(A-M Lewis Inc.)
8810 Tampa Avenue
Northridge, 91324
(213) 349-6600

Place and Gera Inc. (750)
400 E. Brokaw Road
San Jose, 95112
(408) 436-8222

Rawson Drugs and Sundry
  Co. (1,800)
2013 Farallon Drive
San Leandro, 94577
(415) 352-6600

Super Market Sales (550)
1150 Harrison Street
San Francisco, 94103
(415) 621-3344

USCP-Wesco Inc. (500)
4444 Ayers Avenue
Los Angeles, 90023
(213) 269-0292

## Colorado

McLane Wester (600)
3800 Weeling Street
Denver, 80239
(303) 373-4780

## Connecticut

Meyers Supply Inc. (1,200)
P.O. Box 1158
191 Sheridan Drive
Naugatuck, 06770
(203) 723-7413

Star Drug Distributors (2,500)
P.O. Box 449
100 Saw Mill Road
West Haven, 06516
(203) 934-9261

## Florida

Allen Hosiery and Novelty
  Co. (400)
245 W. 21st Street
Hialeah, 33010
(305) 887-1346

Baron Sales Co. (575)
266 N.E. 70th Street
Miami, 33138
(305) 754-4931

Butler Industries Inc. (2,000)
4215 S.W. 34th Street
Orlando, 32818
(305) 648-5373

Sav-A-Stop (4,500)
500 Wells Road
Orange Park, 32073
(904) 264-1281

## Georgia

May and Co. (2,100)
1159 Morrow Industrial
  Boulevard
Morrow, 30260
(404) 961-7044

Merchants Specialty (350)
P.O. Box 1110
224 W. Ashley Street
Douglas, 31533

Serv-A Store (1,000)
5335 Snapfinger Woods Drive
Decatur, 30035
(404) 981-5606

J. S. Smith and Sons (400)
P.O. Box 23
511 Sycamore Street
Waycross, 31501
(912) 283-6747

Southern Merchandise (325)
P.O. Box 638
Statesboro, 30458
(912) 764-6408

## Hawaii

Hawaiian Housewares (1,000)
99-1151 Iwaena Street
Aiea, 96701
(808) 587-0035;
  (800) 456-8000

## Idaho

Albertsons-Sundries Center
  (340)
P.O. Box 7924
Boise, 83707
(208) 375-8930

Slusser Wholesale Co.
  (1,500)
920 Lincoln Road
Idaho Falls, 83401
(208) 523-0775

## Illinois

Commodity Sales (300)
6332 W. Roosevelt Road
Oak Park, 60304
(312) 848-6402

Jaydon Inc. (3,000)
7800 14th Street W.
Rock Island, 61201
(309) 787-4492

Jay-Mac Inc. (300)
430 Meyer Road
Bensenville, 60106
(312) 595-9651

Kempler Sales Co. (500)
3015 W. Lawrence Avenue
Chicago, 60625
(312) 463-0550

Lincolnwood Merchandising
  Co. (1,500)
5359 N. Broadway
Chicago, 60640
(312) 275-2838

Shack Industries (500)
3300 W. Cermak Road
Chicago, 60623
(312) 277-4410

Wait-Cahill Co. (500)
704-32 N. Monroe Street
Decatur, 62522
(217) 422-2334

I. Wolfmark Inc. (500)
775 W. Jackson Boulevard
Chicago, 60606
(312) 782-7560

## Indiana

Dale Sales Co. (600)
P.O. Box 3789
2504 Lynch Road
Evansville, 47736
(812) 464-3611

Food Marketing Corp. (320)
4815 Executive Boulevard
Fort Wayne, 46801
(219) 483-2146

Gayee Sales (300)
P.O. Box 2727
916 Burlington Drive
Muncie, 47302
(317) 289-2143

Lake End Sales Inc. (420)
P.O. Box 1721
6916 Nelson Road
Fort Wayne, 46801
(219) 749-8561

Michiana Merchandising
  (300)
1655 E. 12th Street
Mishawaka, 46544
(219) 259-3784

Richmond Wholesale Co.
  (1,000)
202 N. Cottage Avenue
Goshen, 46526
(219) 533-3155

## Kansas

Fleming General
  Merchandise (1,000)
P.O. Box 1817
7215 S. Topeka Boulevard
Topeka, 66601
(913) 862-2266

## Kentucky

Cumberland Wholesale
  Distributors (300)
P.O. Box 377
419 S. Main Street
Burkesville, 42717
(502) 864-4168

H & N Distributors (500)
1235 Bardstown Road
Louisville, 40264
(502) 458-2954

Knox Cash Jobbers (300)
104 Highway 25 "E"
Barbourville, 40906
(606) 546-3440

## Louisiana

Homer Tobacco Candy and
  Drug (500)
412 E. Main Street
Homer, 71040
(318) 927-3928

Lafayette Drug (600)
220 N. University Avenue
Lafayette, 70502
(318) 233-9041

J. Lane (350)
2620 Midway Avenue
Shreveport, 71108
(318) 635-2127


Rack Service (1,100)
P.O. Box 4727
Monroe, 71211
(318) 322-1446


Triangle Wholesale Drug
  Co. (300)
7501 Westbank Expressway
Marrero, 70072
(504) 347-3232


## Maine

A & M Hackett (300)
P.O. Box 160
Caribou, 04736
(207) 496-3331


The Jayson Co. (1,500)
75 India Street
Portland, 04104
(207) 773-3827


Jayson/Benson & Sullivan
  Co. (1,500)
254 Minot Avenue
Auburn, 04210
(207) 784-2306


Byron H. Smith and Co.
  (630)
54 Perry Road
Auburn, 04210
(207) 942-5531


## Maryland

F. A. Davis and Sons
  (6,000)
111 S. Paca Street
Baltimore, 21230
(301) 685-3900


B. T. Kilmon and Co. (500)
Snow Hill Road
Salisbury, 21801
(301) 749-3226


## Massachusetts

A. Ashkar Sales Co. (308)
10 Crowley Avenue
North Adams, 01247
(413) 663-5301


Cariddi Sales Co. (800)
P.O. Box 446
508 State Road
North Adams, 01247
(413) 663-3723


Godin Stores Inc. (300)
(Godroy Wholesale Co.)
17 Simonds Road
Fitchburg, 01420
(617) 345-6186


Halmar Distributors (300)
49 Garfield Street
Holyoke, 01040
(413) 538-5700


Herman Inc. (1,500)
Avon Industrial Center
Avon, 02322
(617) 587-6300

Millbrook Distributors
(400)
P.O. Box 218
Route 56
Leicester, 01524
(617) 892-8171

## Michigan

Chaffee and Co. (4,000)
12700 Reeck Road
Southgate, 48195
(313) 287-4800

Household Products Co.
(1,000)
2240 Greer Street
Keego Harbor, 48033
(313) 682-1400

Items Galore (1,200)
14235 Frazho Road
Warren, 48089
(313) 774-4800

King Michigan Sundries
(1,200)
1139 Fenway Circle
Fenton, 48430
(313) 629-5464

Payette Distributing Co.
(300)
55 Mt. Veron Avenue N.W.
Grand Rapids, 49504
(616) 459-3258

Sandler Stone Co. (300)
16400 Plymouth Road
Detroit, 48227
(313) 836-4006

Spartan Stores Inc. (435)
P.O. Box 8700
850 76th Street S.W.
Grand Rapids, 49508
(616) 878-2000

## Minnesota

Drug Specialties (500)
127 N.E. 5th Street
Minneapolis, 55413
(612) 379-2844

R & L Distributing Co.
(300)
6800 Shingle Creek Parkway
Brooklyn Center, 55430
(612) 560-6550

Scholl's Inc. (3,000)
P.O. Box 43116
St. Paul, 55164
(612) 636-0892

Somody Supply Inc. (1,000)
P.O. Box 444
800 Highway 23 S.W.
Willmar, 56201
(612) 235-2454

## Mississippi

Dixie Tobacco and Candy
Co. (750)
Main Street
Shaw, 38773
(601) 754-3561

Magnolia Mills Inc. (2,000)
511 30th Avenue
Meridian, 39301
(601) 483-1823

## Missouri

N. A. Buffen Co. (450)
2622 Rock Hill Industrial
   Court
St. Louis, 63144
(314) 968-0355


Wetterau Foods Inc. (600)
701 S. Main Street
Desloge, 63601
(314) 431-4027


## Montana

Sundry Shops (300)
112 Humbolt Loop
Helena, 59601
(406) 442-5470


## Nebraska

Midwest Distributors (800)
10th and Juniata Avenue
Juniata, 68955
(402) 751-2155


## Nevada

Pyramid Dist. Co. (300)
P.O. Box 3516
Reno, 89505
(702) 322-9411


## New Hampshire

T.B.I. Corp. (1,200)
700 E. Industrial Park Drive
Manchester, 03108
(603) 668-6223

## New Jersey

Supermarket Service Corp.
   (950)
2 Paragon Drive
Montvale, 07645
(201) 573-9700


United Super Apparel Inc.
   (2,000)
815 Broad Avenue
Ridgefield, 07657
(201) 943-4320


## New York

D.T.S. Discount Toiletry
   (500)
P.O. Box 121
Richmond Hill, 11419
(516) 248-3718


Lubin Distributors (300)
1545 Mt. Read Boulevard
Rochester, 14606
(716) 458-6024


Sandy Sales Co. (650)
P.O. Box 52
22 N. College Street
Schenectady, 12301
(518) 374-4451


Selecto Products Co. (700)
1 Elm Street
Ardsley, 10502
(914) 693-1300


## North Carolina

C-B Corp. (3,000)
213 S. 49 Highway
Harrisburg, 28075
(704) 455-2165

Coats Distributors (3,500)
Highway 421 W.
Dunn, 28334
(919) 892-8161

Garner Wholesale
    Merchandisers
P.O. Box 1446
Memorial Drive
Greenville, 27834
(919) 758-1189

Johnson Supply Co. (1,300)
P.O. Box 3486
1520 13th Street S.W.
Hickory, 28603
(704) 328-5511

## Ohio

The Friendly Wholesale Co.
    (300)
655 Cushman Street
Wooster, 44691
(216) 264-8222

Meinerding Distributing
    (400)
2336–50 Burnet Road
Cincinnati, 45219
(513) 621-3738

R & A Sales (750)
30600 Carter Street
Solon, 44139
(216) 248-8100

Revco Drug Stores (1,500)
1925 Enterprise Parkway
Twinsburg, 44087
(216) 425-9811

Serv-A-Rack (600)
12430 Elmwood Avenue
Cleveland, 44111
(216) 941-6570

Stratman Distributing (400)
P.O. Box 109
4809 Factory Drive
Fairfield, 40514
(513) 829-8881

Tri-State Rack Services (450)
1st and Hanover Streets
Martins Ferry, 43935
(614) 633-0480

## Oklahoma

Anderson Wholesale Co.
    (1,500)
P.O. Box 69
2211 W. Shawnee
Muskogee, 74401
(918) 682-5569

Oklahoma Drug Sales (650)
P.O. Box 419
310 East "D" Avenue
Lawton, 73502
(405) 355-4430

Spindle Wholesale (500)
2216 W. 14th
Sulphur, 73086
(405) 622-2131

## Oregon

Paul Jackson Wholesale (400)
P.O. Box 1020
1308 N.W. Park Street
Roseburg, 97470
(503) 672-7771

Tom Ray Inc. (350)
13489 S.E. Highway 212
Clackamas, 97015
(503) 655-1348

United Grocers (450)
6433 S.E. Lake Road
Milwaukie, 97222
(503) 653-6330

## Pennsylvania

Linco Drug Co. (500)
4315 Old William Penn
   Highway
Monroeville, 15146
(412) 372-1400

Thrift-Rack (400)
P.O. Box 218
201 W. Church Road
Lancaster, 17603
(717) 299-8908

## South Carolina

Buddin's Inc. (400)
2129 Cherry Road
Rock Hill, 29730
(803) 366-7147

Chapman Drug Service (350)
P.O. Box 378
West Columbia, 29169
(803) 796-1100

Robyn Ann Inc. (450)
2909 Platt Springs Road
West Columbia, 29169
(803) 794-0302

## Tennessee

Budget Distributing (750)
2714 Westwood Drive
Nashville, 37204
(615) 383-7761

Clapp Sales Inc. (375)
2233 Sycamore Drive
Knoxville, 37921
(615) 523-0640

Display Service of Tennessee
   Inc. (300)
P.O. Box 1238
2908 Patrick Avenue
Maryville, 37801
(615) 983-6654

Fraker Sales Co. (1,200)
2233 Sycamore Drive
Knoxville, 37921
(615) 546-9383

Heart To Heart Expressions
   (600)
910 Ben Ellen Road
Nashville, 37216
(615) 226-0674

Leader Specialty Co.
   (1,000)
138 Webster Avenue
Memphis, 38126
(901) 527-8657

Mid States Paper and Notion
   Co. (800)
P.O. Box 8248
810 Cherokee Avenue
Nashville, 37207
(615) 226-1234

Star Sales (5,000)
P.O. Box 1503
1803 N. Central
Knoxville, 37917
(615) 524-0771

## Texas

The Fleming Co. (300)
3400 Can Morton Drive
Dallas, 75236
(214) 298-2444

M-K Housewares (1,000)
1273 Shotwell
Houston, 77020
(713) 676-1901

Mclane Southwest (3,000)
3015 Center Street
Temple, 76501
(817) 778-5585

Sav-A-Stop (1,300)
P.O. Box 30660
6061 Plains Boulevard
Amarillo, 79121
(806) 352-5211

## Virginia

Sav-A-Stop Inc. (2,000)
2001 Apperson Drive
Salem, 24153
(703) 774-4431

## Washington

Central Sales Co. (300)
2986 Cyrus Creek Road
Barboursville, 25504

Mclane/Northwest (750)
4700 100th Street S.W.
Tacoma, 98499
(206) 582-7500

Merchants Supply Inc.
  (350)
P.O. Box 1018
782 Marine Drive
Bellingham, 98227
(206) 733-4700

Northern Merchandise Co.
  (1,000)
15425 N.E. 90th Street
Redmond, 98052
(206) 881-2922

West Coast Grocer (500)
1525 East "D" Street
Tacoma, 98401
(206) 593-3200

## Wisconsin

Constant Distributing Co.
  (1,400)
2120 S. Calhoun Road
New Berlin, 53151
(414) 786-7210

Demars Inc. (500)
219 S. Main Street
Cottage Grove, 53527
(608) 839-4546

E. Z. Gregory Inc. (1,000)
P.O. Box 4268
Madison, 53711
(608) 271-2324

A. J. Robertson Distributing Co. (300)
1929 Vernon Street
Eau Claire, 54701
(715) 834-6651

Scholl Distributing Co. (500)
1003 W. Park Avenue
Chippewa Falls, 54729
(715) 723-7309

## Toy Buyers

### *East Coast*

#### DEPARTMENT STORES

Abraham & Straus
420 Fulton Street
Brooklyn, NY 11201
Toy buyer: Cindy Miklos, (718) 802-7882

Bloomingdale's
59th Street and Lexington Avenue
New York, NY 10022
Toy buyer: Constance Policatti, (212) 705-5674

Hahne & Co.
Broad Street
Newark, NJ 07101
(201) 623-4100

Lord & Taylor
424 Fifth Avenue
New York, NY 10018
Toy buyer: Mary McCormick, (212) 391-3246

Macy's
Broadway and 34th Street
New York, NY 10001
Toy buyer: Joe Meny, (212) 560-3645

May's
Fulton and Bond Sheets
Brooklyn, NY 11201
Toy buyer: Dave Canter, (718) 624-7400

F.A.O. Schwarz
767 Fifth Avenue
New York, NY 10151
Toy buyers: Ian McDermott, Joan Rehfield, Mark Anthony, Connie Van Epps, (212) 758-4344

Sterns Department Stores
Route 4, Bergen Mall
Paramus, NJ 07652
Toy buyer: LeeAnn Gargagliano, (201) 845-2242

#### CHAIN STORES

Affiliated Drug Stores Inc.
15 E. 26th Street
New York, NY 10010
Toy buyer: Richard Glassman, (212) 889-1560

Ames Department Store
2418 Main Street
Rocky Hill, CT 06067
Toy buyers: Bob Coones, Cheryl Landy, Kathy Kester, (203) 563-8234

Associated Chain Drug Stores
330 Seventh Avenue
New York, NY 10011
Toy buyers: Jack Price and
    Anne Kabak (plush and
    stuffed toys), (212) 967-9890

M. H. Lamston Inc.
270 Eighth Avenue
New York, NY 10011
Toy buyer: Marge Flanagan,
    (212) 242-9230

McCrory Stores
2955 E. Market Street
York, PA 17402
Toy buyers: J. D. Cook and
    Larry Scott, (717) 757-8976

S. E. Nichols Inc.
275 Seventh Avenue
New York, NY 10001
Toy buyer: Marvin Schwartz,
    (212) 206-9400

J. C. Penney Co. Inc.
1301 Avenue of the Americas
New York, NY 10019
Toy buyers: Chuck Gage,
    (212) 957-5620;
    J. Carrigan, 957-5623;
    Larry Malvagno, 957-4379;
    Bob Ekinson, buyers'
    assistant, 957-5548

TSS-Seedman's Inc.
104–01 Foster Avenue
Brooklyn, NY 11236
(718) 272-9600

Toys-"Я"-Us Inc.
395 W. Passaic Street
Rochelle Park, NJ 07662
(201) 368-5440

F. W. Woolworth
233 Broadway
New York, NY 10279
Toy buyer: Charles Mullins,
    (212) 553-2000

## RESIDENT BUYERS

Allied Stores Marketing
    Corp.
1120 Avenue of the Americas
New York, NY 10036
(212) 764-2120

Associated Merchandising
    Corp.
1440 Broadway
New York, NY 10018

Frederick Atkins Inc.
1515 Broadway
New York, NY 10036
Toy buyer: Madeline
    Krashinsky, (212)
    840-7000, ext. 351

Atlas Buying Corp.
1515 Broadway
New York, NY 10036
Toy buyer: M. J. Sabatino,
    (212) 730-8000

Independent Retailers
    Syndicate
33 W. 34th Street
New York, NY 10001
Toy buyer: Elise Fuchs,
    (212) 564-4900

Felix Lilienthal & Co.
417 Fifth Avenue
New York, NY 10016
Toy buyer: Liz Hacker,
    (212) 889-9200

May Merchandising
1120 Avenue of the Americas
New York, NY 10036
(212) 704-2654

## Midwest

### DEPARTMENT STORES

Carson Pirie Scott & Co.
1 South State Street
Chicago, IL 60603
Toy buyer: (312) 744-2490

Gateley's People Store
6901 W. 159 Street
Tinley Park, IL 60477
Toy buyer: Jerry Gateley,
    (312) 429-2400

Gold Circle Stores
6121 Huntley Road
Worthington, OH 43085
(614) 438-4365

Marshall Field & Co.
111 North State Street
Chicago, IL 60690
Toy buyer: Elena Diaz, (312)
    781-5655

Neiman-Marcus
Main & Ervay
Dallas, TX 75201
Toy buyer: Ann Stuart
    McKie, (214) 573-5661

Wieboldts Stores
1 North State Street
Chicago, IL 60602
Toy buyer: Daniel Anderson,
    (312) 984-2035

### CHAIN STORES

Ben Franklin Stores
1700 S. Wolf Road
Des Plaines, IL 60018
Toy buyers: Charles Kreichelt
    and Steve Sears,
    (312) 298-8800

Toys Plus Inc.
1600 Heritage Landing,
    Suite 101
St. Charles, MO 6330?
(314) 928-1900

Walgreen Co.
200 Wilmott Road
Deerfield, IL 60015
Toy buyer: Mark Paul
    (312) 940-2500

### MAIL ORDER HOUSES

Montgomery Ward & Co.
619 W. Chicago Avenue
Chicago, IL 60607
Toy buyers: G. T. Maxson,
    (312) 467-2566; B. S.
    Roser, 467-2568; Rita
    Hamilton, 467-2573

Sears, Roebuck & Co.
Sears Tower
Chicago, IL 60684
Toy buyers: Herb Kretz,
    (312) 875-3810; John
    Striet, 875-6069; Bob
    Gerard, 875-6097; Mary
    Kaye, 875-6105

Spiegel
Regency Towers
1515 W. 22nd Street
Oak Brook, IL 60521
Toy buyers: Ron Panek,
   (312) 986-7500, ext. 7701;
   James O'Toole, ext. 7702

## WHOLESALERS

Ace Hardware Corp.
2200 Kensington Court
Oak Brook, IL 60521
(312) 990-6684

Devco Sales Co.
1616 Payne Street
Evanston, IL 60201
Toy buyers: Norm Cotler
   and Karl Pogrund, (312)
   869-3246

M. W. Kasch Co.
5401 W. Donges Bay Road
Mequon, WI 53092
Toy buyers: Tom Ertel and
   Kay Miller, (414) 242-5000

Trost Modelcraft & Hobbies
312 W. 47th Street
Chicago, IL 60632
Toy buyers: Betty and Mike
   Trost, (312) 927-1400

## *West Coast*

## DEPARTMENT STORES

Broadway Department Stores
3880 N. Mission Road
Los Angeles, CA 90031
Toy buyers: Thomas Castle
   and Patti Johnson, (213)
   227-2391

Bullock's
800 South Hope Street
Los Angeles, CA 90017
Toy buyer: Kathryn Kossel,
   (213) 612-5631

The Emporium
835 Market Street
San Francisco, CA 94101
Toy buyer: Barbara Perolini,
   (415) 764-3090

May Co.
6160 Laurel Canyon
   Boulevard
N. Hollywood, CA 91606
Toy buyer: Steve McLean,
   (818) 509-4638

J. W. Robinson Co.
600 W. 7th Street
Los Angeles, CA 90017
Toy buyer: Jean Schwider,
   (213) 488-6024

## WHOLESALERS

Austin Merle Co.
5840 E. Slauson Avenue
Los Angeles, CA 90040
Toy buyer: (213) 726-9700

California Hobby Distributors
415 S. Palm Avenue
Alhambra, CA 91803
Hobby buyer: Franklyn Veir,
   (818) 289-8857

Federal Wholesale Toy Co.
14407 Alondra Boulevard
La Mirada, CA 90638
Toy buyers: Milton Miller,
   Louis Miller, Robert
   Pennes, William Bernstein,
   Richard Miller, Leslie
   Mendelsohn, Edwin
   Bernstein, (213) 587-5071

J & S Distributing Co.
711 E. Rosecrans Avenue
Los Angeles, CA 90059
Toy buyer: Gail Cavanagh,
 (213) 321-4055

New York Merchandise Co.
5505 E. Olympic Boulevard
Los Angeles, CA 90022
Toy buyer: Max Fadkin,
 (213) 723-9501

Oakland Toy Co.
16500 Worthley Drive
San Lorenzo, CA 94580
Toy buyer: George Alton,
 (415) 351-7993

Pacific Model Distributors
7317 Compton Boulevard
Paramount, CA 90723
Toy buyer: Mel H. Walker,
 (213) 630-5222

# Appendix 4

## Trade Show Schedule

If you want to hit a lot of industry people at the same time, a trade show is the place to do it. A trade show is a convention where sellers, buyers, and distributors of a particular industry gather to impress each other, drink a lot of martinis, and make deals. To be able to exhibit at a trade show, you must contact the sponsoring organization. (Usually the name gives it away. Those of you with the world's next Vegematic would want the International Housewares Exposition in Chicago, run by the National Housewares Manufacturers' Association.) If you just want to go, no advance notice is necessary, but a business card will help get you in the door.

### January 1990

Winter Consumer Electronics Show
Las Vegas Convention Center, 6-9
Contact: CES
(202) 457-4919

National China, Glass and Collectibles
Javits Center, New York City, 7-10
Contact: George Little Management Company
(212) 686-6070

Hong Kong Toy and Games Fair
Hong Kong Convention and Exhibition Centre, 10-13
Contact: Hong Kong Trade Development Council
(212) 838-8688

Harrogate International Toy Fair
Contact: Harrogate International Toy Fair, 13-18
8/9 Upper Street, Islington, London
N1 OPP, England

Washington Gift Show
Washington Convention Center, D.C., 7-10
Contact: George Little Management Company
(212) 686-6070

Transworld Housewares and Variety Exhibit
O'Hare Expo Center, Rosemont/Chicago, 12-16
Contact: Transworld Exhibits Inc.
(312) 442-8434

New York International Gift Fair
Including Accent on Design, American Crafts and the Pier Group
Javits Center, New York City, 27-31
Contact: George Little Management Company
(212) 686-6070

British Toy and Hobby Fair
Earl's Court, 27-31
Contact: British Toy Fairs International
80 Camberwell Rd., London, England SE5 OEG

Canadian Toy Fair
Toronto, 28-Feb. 2.
Canadian Toy Manufacturer's Association
Box 294, Kleinburg, Ontario LOJ ICO

Paris International Toy Fair
Paris-Nord International Exhibition Center, 31-Feb. 6
Contact: (212) 869-1720

IIIA Convention and Trade Show
Dallas Convention Center, 23-28
Contact: IIIA
(201) 794-1133

## February 1990

Chicago Gift Show (winter)
McCormack Place North, Chicago, 4-8
Contact: George Little Management Company
(212) 686-6070

National Back To School Merchandise Show
Javits Center, New York City, 11-13
Contact: Thalheim Expositions
(516) 627-4000

International Toy Fair
Nurnberg-Messezentrum,
West Germany, 8-14
Contact: International
Speilwarenmesse, EGmbH
8500 Nurnberg

American International Toy
Fair
New York, 12-21
Contact: Toy Manufacturers
of America
(212) 675-1141

Valencia Toy Fair
Valencia, Spain, 15-20
Contact: Feria del Jugete,
y articulos para la
infancia
Llano del real 2-Apartado
476, Valencia, Spain

Toytech
New York Penta, 20-21
Contact: Charles A. Dec
(212) 418-4118

Variety Merchandise Show
Javits Center, New York
City, 17-20
Contact: Thalheim
Expositions
(516) 627-4000

Atlantic City Gift Show
Atlantic City, NJ, 25-28
Contact for Location: George
Little Management
Company
(212) 686-6070

## March 1990

Dallas Toy Fair
Dallas Market Center, 11-14
(214) 655-6100

Transworld Housewares and
Variety Exhibit
O'Hare Expo Center,
Rosemont/Chicago, 23-27
Contact: Transworld Exhibits
Inc.
(312) 442-8434

National Halloween and
Costume Show
O'Hare Expo Center,
Rosemont/Chicago, 23-27
Contact: Transworld Exhibits
Inc.
(312) 442-8434

National Party Show
O'Hare Expo Center,
Rosemont/Chicago, 23-27
Contact: Transworld Exhibits
Inc.
(312) 442-8434

Boston Gift Show
Bayside Exposition and
World Trade Center, 24-28
Contact: George Little
Management Company
(212) 686-6070

San Diego Gift and Stationery
Show
San Diego Convention and
Performing Arts Center,
25-28
Contact: George Little
Management Company
(212) 686-6070

## April 1990

San Francisco Gourmet Show
Mascone Center, 22-25
Contact: George Little
    Management Company
(212) 686-6070

San Francisco Food and
    Beverage Show
Civic Auditorium and
    Brooks Hall, 22-24
Contact: George Little
    Management Company
(212) 686-6070

Premium Incentive Show
Javits Center, New York
    City, 30-May 3
Contact: Thalheim Expositions
(516) 627-4000

## May 1990

International Contemporary
    Furniture Fair
Javits Center, New York
    City, 20-22
Contact: George Little
    Management Company
(212) 686-6070

National Stationery Show
Javits Center, New York
    City, 20-23
Contact: George Little
    Management Company
(212) 686-6070

SURTEX
Javits Center, New York
    City, 21-23
Contact: George Little
    Management Company
(212) 686-6070

## June 1990

The Mid-Year Variety and
    Merchandise Show
Javits Center, New York
    City, 6-12
Contact: Thalheim
    Expositions
(516) 627-4000

Tokyo Toy Fair
No. 22-4 Higashi-Komagata
Sumida-Ku Tokyo, Japan,
    15-18
Contact: Japan International
    Toy Fair Association

## July 1990

Transworld Housewares and
    Variety Exhibit
O'Hare Expo Center,
    Rosemont/Chicago, 6-10
Contact: Transworld Exhibits
    Inc.
(312) 442-8434

Chicago Gift Show
McCormack Place North,
    15-19
Contact: George Little
    Management Company
(212) 686-6070

## August 1990

New York International
    Gift Fair
Including Accent on Design,
American and International
    Crafts and the Pier Group
Javits Center, New York
    City, 11-15
Contact: George Little
    Management Company
(212) 686-6070

## September 1990

The National Merchandise Show
Javits Center, New York City, 8-11
Contact: Thalheim Expositions
(516) 627-4000

New York Gourmet Show
Javits Center, New York City, 9-12
Contact: George Little Management Company
(212) 686-6070

SITOY '89
361-1 2-ka Hankang-ro Yongsan-ku
Seoul, Korea, 23-26.
Contact: Korea Toy Industry Cooperative

Asian International Toy and Gift Fair
Ocean Terminal, Tsimshatsui, Kowloon Hong Kong, 25-27
Contact: Raymond Chin, Cahners Exposition Group, 1507 Shun Tak Centre, 200 Connaught Rd., Central Hong Kong

Dallas Toy Fair
Dallas Market Center, 25-27
Contact: (214) 655-6100

Taipei International Toy Fair
Taipei, 27-Oct. 1
Contact: CETRA Exhibition Dept.
5 Hsinyi Section 5
Taipei, 10509 Taiwan Republic of China

## October 1990

Transworld Housewares and Variety Exhibit
O'Hare Expo Center, Rosemont/Chicago, 26-30
Contact: Transworld Exhibits Inc.
(312) 442-8434

## November 1990

Hotel and Motel Show
Javits Center, New York City, 10-13
Contact: George Little Management Company
(212) 686-6070

## February 1991

National Back To School Merchandise Show
Javits Center, New York City, 9-11
Contact: Thalheim Expositions
(516) 627-4000

Toy Manufacturers of America
Toy Fair, New York, 11-20
(212) 675-1141

Variety Merchandise Show
Javits Center, New York City, 16-19
Contact: Thalheim Expositions
(516) 627-4000

## May 1991

Premium Incentive Show
Javits Center, New York
  City, 6-9
Contact: Thalheim
  Expositions
(516) 627-4000

## June 1991

The Mid-Year Variety and
  Merchandise Show
Javits Center, New York
  City, 15-18
Contact: Thalheim
  Expositions
(516) 627-4000

## September 1991

The National Merchandise
  Show
Javits Center, New York
  City, 21-24
Contact: Thalheim
  Expositions
(516) 627-4000

# Appendix 5

# Trade Associations

If it's sold in the United States, it has its own trade association to promote itself. That's why the margarine manufacturers, the oil jobbers, the valve manufacturers, and others have all banded together into organizations with bylaws and annual meetings. Whatever it is you have to push, there is probably a prefabricated organization ready and willing to help you. From Christmas ornaments to stuffed dolls, you can find it in this list. If you can't, look in the Yellow Pages under "Associations."

American Importers and
 Exporters Association
11 West 42nd Street
New York, NY 10036
(212) 944-2230

Association for the
 Anthropological Study
 of Play
Children's Research
 Center
Champaign, IL 61820
(217) 333-6434

Bicycle Manufacturers'
 Association
1055 Thomas Jefferson
 Street NW
Washington, DC 20007
(202) 333-4052

Children's Advertising
 Review Unit
Council of Better
 Business Bureaus
845 Third Avenue
New York, NY 10022
(212) 754-1353

Electronic Industries'
Association
2001 I Street NW
Washington, DC 20006
(202) 457-4900

Exhibit Designers' and
Producers' Association
Washington, DC
(202) 393-2001

Gift Association of America
1511 K Street NW, Suite 716
Washington, DC 20005
(202) 638-6080

Golf Manufacturers' and
Distributors' Association
P.O. Box 37324
Cincinnati, OH 45222
(513) 631-4400

Hobby Industries of America
319 East 54th Street
P.O. Box 348
Elmwood Park, NJ 07407
(201) 234-9155

International Exhibitors'
Association
Annandale, VA
(703) 941-3725

Licensing Industry
Merchandisers' Association
350 Fifth Avenue
New York, NY 10118
(212) 794-1133

National Association of
Doll and Stuffed Toy
Manufacturers
605 Third Avenue, 18th Floor
New York, NY 10158
(212) 916-9200

National Association of
Miniature Enthusiasts
P.O. Box 2621
Anaheim, CA 92804
(714) 529-0900

National Mass Retailing
Institute
570 Seventh Avenue
New York, NY 10018
(212) 354-6600

National Ornament and
Electric Lights
15 East 26th Street
New York, NY 10010
(212) 889-8343

National Tabletop
Association (Gifts)
41 Madison Avenue,
Suite 7D
New York, NY 10010
(212) 481-3830

Point-of-Purchase
Advertising Institute
2 Executive Drive
Fort Lee, NJ 07024
(201) 585-8400

Society of Plastics Industry
355 Lexington Avenue
New York, NY 10017
(212) 370-7340

Souvenir and Novelty Trade
Association
401 N. Broad Street,
Suite 226
Philadelphia, PA 19108
(215) 925-9744

Sporting Goods
 Manufacturers Association
200 Castlewood Drive
North Palm Beach, FL 33408
(305) 842-4100

Toy Manufacturers of
 America Inc.
Room 740
200 Fifth Avenue
New York, NY 10010
(212) 675-1141

Toy Wholesalers Association
 of America
66 East Main Street
Moorestown, NJ 08057
(609) 234-9155

Trade Show Bureau
East Orleans, MA
(617) 240-0177

Trade Show Services
 Association
Broadview, IL
(312) 450-6780

USA Toy Library
 Association
104 Wilmot, Suite 201
Deerfield, IL 60015
(312) 940-8800